Ms. Jeri Ferris
2183 Nighthawk Ln
Lincoln CA 95648

D0473872

DISCIPLESHIP

The Road Less Taken

DISCIPLESHIP

The Road Less Taken

GREG LAURIE

KERYGMA™ PUBLISHING

ALLEN DAVID BOOKS

Discipleship: The Road Less Taken

Copyright © 2009 by Greg Laurie. All rights reserved.

Unless otherwise indicated, all Scripture quotations are taken from the New King James Version. Copyright © 1982 by Thomas Nelson, Inc. Used by permission. All rights reserved.

Scripture quotations marked (NIV) are taken from THE HOLY BIBLE, NEW INTERNATIONAL VERSION (North American Edition). Copyright © 1973, 1978, 1984 by International Bible Society. Used by permission of Zondervan Publishing House.

Scripture quotations marked (NLT) are taken from the Holy Bible, New Living Translation, copyright 1996, 2004. Used by permission of Tyndale House Publishers, Inc., Wheaton, Illinois 60189. All rights reserved.

Scripture quotations marked (KJV) are taken from the Holy Bible, King James Version. Public domain in the United States.

Scripture quotations marked (AMP) are taken from THE AMPLIFIED BIBLE, Old Testament copyright © 1965, 1987 by the Zondervan Corporation. The Amplified New Testament copyright © 1958, 1987 by the Lockman Foundation. Used by permission.

ISBN: 978-0-9801831-6-0
Published by: Kerygma Publishing—Allen David Books, Dana Point, California
Coordination: FM Management, Ltd.
Editor: Karla Pedrow
Cover design: Ross Geerdes
Interior design: Highgate Cross+Cathey
Production: Highgate Cross+Cathey
Printed in the United States of America

Portions of this book previously published as
Discipleship: Giving God Your Best
Copyright © Harvest House Publishers, Eugene, Ore., 1993

*To Jonathan Allen Laurie, a growing disciple of
Jesus Christ of whom I am very proud.*

CONTENTS

I am indebted to G. Campbell Morgan and J. Dwight Pentecost for their books on the subject of discipleship.

Introduction

What comes to mind when you hear the word "disciple"? Maybe you think of the twelve disciples who followed Jesus Christ through the Judean wilderness and the dusty streets of Jerusalem. Or perhaps it brings to mind a highly disciplined individual who follows something or someone devotedly. But when you think of a disciple, do you think of yourself? Do you consider yourself a disciple of Jesus Christ? Do you know what it means to be one?

True discipleship is getting back to the Christian life as it was meant to be lived. In one sense, we might call it radical Christian living. In our age of personal rights and independent thinking, discipleship seems like a radical concept. And when we compare it to the anemic substitute that is often offered as the Christian life today, it most certainly is radical. But in the biblical sense, radical Christian living is really normal Christian living. The first-century believers who followed Jesus Christ fully were men and women who turned their world upside down. They lived the Christian life as Jesus had presented it to them personally.

The good news is that we, too, can participate in this lifestyle. The purpose of this book is to call us back to New Testament Christian living, to embrace discipleship as Jesus taught it, as the disciples apprehended it, and as the early church lived it.

It is my conviction that every disciple is a believer, but not every believer is necessarily a disciple. Anything short of discipleship is settling for less than what God desires. Jesus clearly calls all believers to be disciples. But when we fail to respond to His call, we fall short of His perfect will and miss out on living the Christian life as it was truly meant to be lived.

What we often perceive as the Christian life is, in many ways, not what the Bible really teaches. We need to ask ourselves whether we are living the Christian life as it was meant to be lived. Is your life challenging? Exciting? Does it have purpose and direction? Or do you find yourself depressed and afraid? If your Christian experience is dull, unfulfilling, or even boring, then it is time to seriously examine the statements of Jesus concerning discipleship.

Ray Stedman wrote, "The chief mark of the Christian ought to be the absence of fear and the presence of joy. We have often quoted the description of a Christian as one who is: completely fearless, continually cheerful, and constantly in trouble. It is that presence of joy and absence of fear that marks our genuine Christianity and proves that we really are what we claim to be."[1]

That is what the world needs more of today: Christians who are full of joy and completely fearless. In short, we need disciples.

After all, how can we expect to fulfill the Great Commission to go into all the world and make disciples if we don't even know what it is to be a disciple? As the saying goes, it takes one to make one.

I want to help you understand what discipleship really is—as presented by Jesus Christ—so that you can implement it in your life through the help of the Holy Spirit. In the following chapters we will look at the essentials for being a disciple of Jesus Christ in the twenty-first century.

Make no mistake about it. If you live this Christian life as Jesus taught it and as the early church lived it, you will enjoy life to its fullest as you walk in the center of the perfect will of God. So join me in this spiritual odyssey as we follow the words of Jesus concerning the life of a true disciple. As we go through these steps to discipleship as laid out by Jesus, it is my prayer that you will seriously consider them and, most importantly, apply them to your life. If you do, the world may never be the same.

G.L.

CHAPTER ONE
Are You His Disciple?

As He passed by, He saw Levi the son of Alphaeus sitting at the tax office. And He said to him, "Follow Me." So he arose and followed Him. (Mark 2:14)

The Christian life is the greatest life there is. Having lived on both sides of the fence, I can say without a doubt that it is the better way to live—by a long shot. There is really no comparison at all. It really is, as the Bible says, a turning from "darkness to light, and from the power of Satan to God" (Acts 26:18). I wasn't brought up to pray, read the Bible, or go to church. I had pretty much experienced all the world has to offer, which sent me on a search that ultimately led me to a relationship with God through Jesus Christ.

Instead of turmoil, I found peace. Instead of misery, I felt joy. Instead of hate, I had love. And most importantly, instead of a future separated from God in a place called hell, I have the hope of being in His presence forever in heaven.

But the Christian life is more than just praying a prayer and getting "fire insurance," so to speak. It is following Jesus Christ not only as your Savior, but also as your Lord. It is having Him not only as your friend, but as your master.

The problem is there are a lot of Christians who have never grown up spiritually. They made an initial commitment to Jesus, yet they have never really understood what it means to be a committed follower of Christ. In short, they have not responded to what the Bible calls discipleship. They are still acting like spiritual infants.

I have two granddaughters, and so of course I think babies are cute. But I also realize that babies are a lot of work. For example, just teaching a baby how to eat is a process. When they are young, they need to be nursed or fed their formula. Next they work up to baby food. When they get their teeth, they can begin eating baby-sized bites of food that have been carefully cut up for them. Then they learn how to use a spoon and other utensils. Eventually they learn how to cut their food, eat their food, and ultimately, prepare their food. It is called growing up.

In the same way, there are some people who have never grown up spiritually. Yet the Bible warns us, "So let us stop going over the basic teachings about Christ again and again. Let us go on instead and become mature in our understanding" (Heb. 6:1 NLT). There is a place for teaching and preaching. God has equipped pastors and teachers to build up believers "so we will no longer be infants, tossed back and forth by the waves, and blown here and there by every wind of teaching and by the cunning and craftiness of men in their deceitful scheming" (Eph. 4:14 NIV). We need to grow up spiritually, mature as believers, and be real disciples.

Requirements for a Disciple

Early in His earthly ministry, Jesus called out to a tax collector named Levi (Matthew), "Follow Me!" (Mark 2:14). Understanding just what Jesus meant by these words will help us get a better picture of what a disciple is. From the original Greek, "Follow Me" may be better translated "follow *with* Me." In other words, Jesus promises to be our companion and friend as we continually and consistently walk the same road with Him.

So what criteria must we meet, what conditions must be fulfilled to be rightfully called by the title of a disciple?

Jesus laid out the requirements of discipleship in Luke 14. He tells us what we need to do to really be His disciple. He addressed these words to a massive group of people that was beginning to follow Him. But to fully understand why Jesus made the statements He did, we must first set the scene at this time in His ministry.

Jesus was at the peak of His popularity at this point in His ministry. Immense crowds thronged Him wherever He went. If you wanted to get near Jesus, you needed as much determination as blind Bartimaeus, who screamed out for Jesus, much to the dismay of the disciples. Or you needed the faith and persistence of the sick woman who reasoned that if she could just touch the Lord in some way, she would be healed.

Clearly, Jesus was greatly admired for His dramatic miracles and insightful teaching. He had become enormously popular among the common people of that time, elevating the outcasts of society and assuring them of God's love, while repeatedly blasting the religious hypocrites of His day.

He was admired, but He wasn't necessarily being followed. And as He looked out on the huge multitude of observers, He could clearly see that these people really didn't know what they were doing. Jesus could see that they didn't understand what it really meant to be His true disciples. So He challenged them. Although His pointed statement was directed to the fascinated multitudes, it is still relevant for us today:

"If anyone comes to Me and does not hate his father and mother, wife and children, brothers and sisters, yes, and his own life also, he cannot be My disciple. And whoever does not bear his cross and come after Me cannot be My disciple. For which of you, intending to build a tower, does not sit down first and count the cost, whether he has enough to finish it? . . . So likewise, whoever of you does

not forsake all that he has cannot be My disciple."
(Luke 14:26–28, 33)

These were perhaps the most solemn and searching words
that ever fell from Jesus' lips. Jesus wasn't calling people to a
marginal belief in Him; He was looking for complete and total
commitment. He was looking for people whom He could call
"disciples." Jesus is still asking us to step out from the multitude,
from the fair-weather followers, from the fickle people to be real
disciples.

He saw a problem developing that we still have with us: people
who respond only to certain aspects of His message. They were pick-
ing and choosing what appealed to them and pretty much ignoring
the rest, not unlike what people do today. So He determined that it
was time to clearly lay out the requirements of following Him, the
true cost of discipleship. Three times in this short passage, He points
out that if you do not do these things, you "cannot be My disciple."
These are absolute prerequisites. And this is the one and only time
He explained the severity of His terms.

Priorities for a Disciple

Foundational to discipleship is loving God more than anyone or
anything else. Jesus said, "If anyone comes to Me and does not hate
his father and mother, wife and children, brothers and sisters, yes,
and his own life also, he cannot be My disciple" (Luke 14:26). A statement like that sounds shocking. But as we balance this verse with
other Scripture, we know clearly Jesus is not commanding the hatred
of people, especially members of our own family. Why would God
tell us to honor our fathers and mothers and also demand that we
hate them? Jesus even told us to "love [our] enemies" (Matt. 5:44), so
we need to get the big picture here.

In context, Jesus was not saying we should hate people, per se.
Essentially He was saying that we should love God more than anyone

or anything else—so much so that our love for those people or things would seem like hatred in comparison.

Jesus was basically saying, "If you want to be my disciple, then love me more than anyone or anything else." It makes perfect sense when you think about it. If you want to live your Christian life to its fullest, then love Jesus more than anyone or anything else.

People have been kept back from following Jesus by their fear of what others might think. They know that if they give their life to Christ, they will lose a lot of so-called friends. If they give their life to Christ, it would mean the end of a relationship. If they give their life to Christ, it would cause friction in their home. That is what holds them back. But Jesus says, "If you really want to be my disciple, you must love me more than anyone or anything else."

In Luke 9 we find the story of a man whom Jesus called to follow Him, but he said, "Lord, let me first go and bury my father" (v. 59).

Jesus told him, "Let the dead bury their own dead, but you go and preach the kingdom of God" (v. 60).

It is easy to read this and think, *What is with that? The guy's father is lying dead, and Jesus says, "Forget about him. He will bury himself. Let's get out of here"?* That is not what was happening, of course. The man was employing a common expression in that culture that meant he wanted to wait until his parents had passed on. In other words he was saying, "When it easier and more convenient, I will do it. Lord, I would like to follow You, but I want to wait until my parents grow old and die. Then, when it fits into my schedule a little better, I will do it." It would be like saying, "I want to follow You, but I don't want it to cause any problems in my relationships. I don't want any friction. I am just not going to do it."

Here is what it comes down to: You either will have harmony with God and friction with people, or you will have harmony with people and friction with God. If you are living the way that God wants you to live, then it is going to seriously bother some people. You need to know that. Jesus said, "Woe to you when all men speak well of you, for that is how their fathers treated the false prophets" (Luke 6:26 NIV). If you are really a follower of Jesus Christ and living as you ought to, there are going to be certain people that don't like you for that reason alone. Don't be hurt by that. Understand it is par for the course. As Jesus said, " 'A servant is not greater than his master.' If they persecuted Me, they will also persecute you" (John 15:20 NIV).

A disciple loves God more than anyone or anything else.

The Cross and the Disciple

Jesus underscored the importance of commitment on the part of a disciple when He referred to the cross. He said, "Whoever does not bear his cross and come after Me cannot be My disciple" (verse 47), and "Then He said to them all, 'If anyone desires to come after Me, let him deny himself, and take up his cross daily, and follow Me. For whoever desires to save his life will lose it, but whoever loses his life for My sake will save it' " (Luke 9:23–24).

Today, the cross has been largely stripped of its original meaning. Shrouded in tradition, it has become a symbol of many things, from a religious icon to an ornate piece of jewelry, studded in diamonds or pearls. Yet the real cross of history was a hated, despised symbol—the symbol of a very cruel death. The Romans reserved this form of torture and execution for the lowest of criminals.

Today we wouldn't expect to see many diamond-studded guillotines or electric chairs hanging around people's necks. They are symbols of death, symbols of shame. The cross was the same thing. When a man carried his cross on the streets of Jerusalem, it was well-known that he was about to die. The convicted criminal would be driven outside the city, nailed to that cross, and placed by the roadside where everyone coming in and out of the city would see him.

So when Jesus said, "If you want to be My disciple, take up your cross," He intentionally chose an attention-getting, even despicable symbol of torture and rejection to illustrate what it means to follow Him. The cross symbolizes one thing: death. And in this context it means dying to self.

Sometimes people identify whatever problem, difficult relationship, or obstacle they have as their "cross to bear." But that is not what bearing the cross means. For disciples, it means that wherever Jesus directs, they should be willing to go. Obviously, this is not an appealing message to many. Satan made an accurate statement of humanity when he said, "All that a man has will he give for his life" (Job 2:4). In other words, he knows that when the chips are down, people will give up everything to stay alive, to preserve themselves.

Jesus was definitely not advocating what I call "easy be-lievism." Far too often we hear, "Just ask Jesus into your heart. He'll make you a happier person. Let God be your copilot." Some will falsely assert that you will become wealthier or healthier once you are a Christian. But that is not the Christianity of the New Testament.

God does not offer himself to us as some celestial big brother or good buddy. The bottom line is that God is absolutely holy and perfect, and we have all sinned horribly against Him. But God, in His great love, bridged the tremendous gap that sin produced, and He sent His own dear Son to die on the cross for us. To receive Him into our lives, we must not only believe in Him, but we must also turn from our sins and follow Him as both our Savior and Lord.

General William Booth, founder of the Salvation Army, wrote of the dangers he saw facing the message of the gospel in the twentieth century. Among other things, he saw a "gospel" that would present Christianity without Christ, forgiveness without repentance, salvation without regeneration, and heaven without hell. And isn't that what we often hear substituted for the true gospel today?

To deny yourself, take up the cross daily, and follow Jesus Christ flies in the face of self-love, which is so widely accepted today, even in the church. We hear a great deal about "self-worth," "self-image," and "self-esteem," yet this shouldn't surprise us, because the Bible warns us that narcissistic attitudes will be prevalent in the days before Christ's return:

> But mark this: There will be terrible times in the last days. People will be *lovers of themselves*, lovers of money, boastful, proud, abusive, disobedient to their parents, ungrateful, unholy, without love, unforgiving, slanderous, without self-control, brutal, not lovers of the good, treacherous, rash, conceited, lovers of pleasure rather than lovers of God—having a form of godliness but denying its power.... (2 Tim. 3:1–5 NIV, emphasis added)

What an accurate description of our times. As we look at our nation and see a society that is coming apart at the seams, we must realize that America's only hope is a nationwide revival.

God gives us His recipe for revival in 2 Chronicles 7:14: "If My people who are called by My name will humble themselves, and pray and seek My face, and turn from their wicked ways, then I will hear from heaven, and will forgive their sin and heal their land."

One of the first conditions we must meet to see our sins forgiven and our land healed is found in the beginning of this passage: "If my people . . . pray." Of the twelve Hebrew words employed to express the single verb "to pray," the one used here means to "judge self habitually"—not to love yourself or to esteem yourself, but to judge yourself . . . habitually.

This is what Jesus means when He tells us to deny ourselves. Discipleship involves commitment. Although discipline is not an appealing word or idea for many of us, it is essential to being a disciple of Jesus Christ. It requires setting aside our aims, goals, ambitions, or desires in life. It involves giving up our own will and rights.

Jesus underscored this when He said, "So likewise, whoever of you does not forsake all that he has cannot be My disciple." (Luke 14:33). This does not mean that to live the life of a disciple, one must take a vow of poverty and give everything away. Jesus meant that we are to surrender our claim to our possessions. In other words, we are not to be possessed by possessions.

The only "obsession" a disciple should have is with Jesus Christ. *He* must be the most important pursuit in our lives. He must be more important than our career or our personal happiness. In fact, we never will find personal happiness until we are fully committed to Christ. Personal happiness is a byproduct of knowing Him: "Happy are the people whose God is the Lord!" (Ps. 144:15).

As Samuel Rutherford said, "The cross of Christ is the sweetest burden that I ever bore." The truth is that when you die to yourself, you find yourself. When you lay aside personal goals, desires, and ambitions, that is when God will reveal the desires, ambitions, and goals that He has for you. This is what the apostle Paul meant when he said, "I have been crucified with Christ; it is no longer I who live, but Christ lives in me" (Gal. 2:20).

Are you bearing the cross right now and following Jesus? For some people, it may mean the suffering of persecution. It may mean a major change in lifestyle. It may cost them friends. To others it could even mean dying for the faith. Whatever the case, bearing the cross will affect and influence every aspect of your life.

Until we recognize that everything we have belongs to Jesus, we are not His disciples. If we are aware of God's will for our lives, but unwilling to go in the direction God wants us to go, then we are not His disciples.

From Curious to Committed

In his insightful book on discipleship, J. Dwight Pentecost writes about the idea of radical Christian living, or true discipleship. He sums it up in three simple words: curious, convinced, and committed.

When Jesus performed His first miracle, or sign, of turning water into wine, the disciples had gone from curious to convinced—convinced that He was an extraordinary person, perhaps even the Messiah: "This beginning of signs Jesus did in Cana of Galilee, and manifested His glory; and His disciples believed in Him" (John 2:11).

When we first see or hear of Jesus Christ, we are curious. Listening to what He said, learning of His life and the miracles attributed to Him, and hearing what others say about Him are obvious attractions—just like they were for the multitudes that surrounded Him when He walked this earth. But there comes a time when we must step over the line of being curious to becoming convinced. And I would venture to say that many who attend church today have never really crossed that line. They are curious, but nothing more. They are attracted to the message, and maybe even to the Christian life, but they are not fully convinced it is true.

These people are like the multitudes after Jesus fed the five thousand with only five loaves of bread and two fish. After He performed this miracle, His popularity soared. Word on the street probably was that if you wanted a free meal, then follow Jesus of Nazareth. There's no doubt that thousands came to hear Him speak, but many were most likely there because of their empty stomachs—not their empty hearts. They were interested in Jesus' message as long as it took care of their temporary needs and as long as it was convenient, which becomes clear in their response to His message. After Jesus gave a very difficult series of teachings on commitment and sacrifice, these so-called followers were repulsed by it and turned away. Then Jesus turned to His disciples and asked if they wanted to leave als

Peter responded, "Lord to whom shall we go? You h words of eternal life. Also we have come to believe and know that You are the Christ, the Son of the living God" (John 6:68–69). The curious went home, but the convinced stuck with Him.

But something more needed to be developed in their belief. They needed to go from being convinced to being committed.

At Caesarea Philippi, Jesus asked the disciples, "Who do men say that I, the Son of Man, am?" (Matt. 16:13). They replied that many thought Jesus to be John the Baptist, while others thought He might be Elijah or even Jeremiah.

Then Jesus asked, "But who do you say that I am?" (v. 15).

Up to this point, the answers He had heard were those of the curious. Then a convinced disciple named Simon Peter stood up and made a step toward being committed. He replied, "You are the Christ, the Son of the living God" (v. 16). Peter had passed from being curious and convinced to being totally and completely committed.

Where do you stand? Are you merely curious? Or perhaps even convinced? Have you made that step of faith to being committed? You become a disciple in the biblical sense only when you are totally and completely committed to Jesus Christ and His Word.

The Results of Discipleship

John's Gospel contains three important verses that will help us understand what it means to be a disciple. They provide us with three evidences, or results of, discipleship.

Result 1: You will bear fruit. In John 15:8, the cornerstone verse for this chapter, Jesus said, "By this My Father is glorified, that you bear much fruit; so you will be My disciples." If you are a true disciple, then you will bear fruit. This means your life will display practical results as you follow Jesus.

Result 2: You will study and obey God's Word. The second characteristic of a disciple is found in John 8:31, where Jesus said,

"If you abide in My word, you are My disciples indeed." If you are a true disciple, you will study and obey God's Word. Disciples of Jesus will be students of Scripture and will walk according to its teaching.

Result 3: You will love one another. A third trademark of a disciple is found in John 13:35. Jesus said, "By this all will know that you are My disciples, if you have love one for another." As a true disciple, your life not only will be characterized by practical results and a hunger for Scripture, but you also will have love for others—especially those who are fellow Christians. Without all of these characteristics, you cannot really claim to be His disciple.

Commitment Is Key

Are you His disciple today? Perhaps you are still just curious, or only slightly convinced. Maybe you are convinced but haven't overcome that final hurdle of commitment. Until you reach that point, you cannot truly be called His disciple.

A true disciple who desires to live a radical Christian life must anchor himself in Romans 12:1: "I beseech you therefore, brethren, by the mercies of God, that you present your bodies a living sacrifice, holy, acceptable to God, which is your reasonable service."

In the Jewish wedding ceremony, the moment at which the father of the bride gave his daughter's hand to the bridegroom was called the presentation. In the same way, God wants us to present ourselves to Him.

Paul, in the chapters leading up to Romans 12, outlines all that God had done for us. Now he says, "In light of all this, I urge you, by the mercies of God, because of what He has done for you, to present yourself to Him as a living sacrifice" (v. 1, author's paraphrase). Paul's idea of discipleship is not just giving intellectual acknowledgment to Jesus as God; it includes obedience and sacrifice.

Do you want to be more than just curious about Jesus? If so, there needs to be a commitment on your part. The requirements of discipleship are different than the requirements of salvation. To be a Christian, you need to believe in Jesus Christ, whom God sent, and then you will receive eternal life through Him. It is a gift. To be a disciple is to take up the cross daily and follow Him, making His will your will. It is a commitment.

Jesus is looking for disciples, not just people to be called Christians in name only. Rather, He is looking for those who will step forward and commit their lives to becoming disciples. Jesus has plenty of fair-weather followers today, people who follow Him when it's convenient, when it's socially or economically advantageous, or when they are in the mood. But when a crisis, persecution, or difficulty comes, they throw in the towel and turn away.

Every disciple is a Christian, but not every Christian is necessarily a disciple. Do you want to be more than curious about Jesus—and more than convinced? Then commit your life to Him as a disciple, and discover what radical Christian living is all about!

Perhaps a commitment like this seems too difficult right now. Remember, if God asks you to do something, He will give you the strength to do it. God's calling is God's enabling. As Philippians 2:13 tells us, "For it is God who works in you both to will and to do for His good pleasure."

That is our guarantee. God will be our enabler. It doesn't take great knowledge. It doesn't take great ability. It only takes our availability.

However, there are no shortcuts on the road of discipleship. There is no secret I can reveal that will replace years of walking with God and being conformed to His image. We live in an age where technology has made it possible to get everything quickly. We have e-mail, instant messaging, Facebook, and Twitter. We simply don't want to take time for certain things, and this impatience carries over into our spiritual lives as well. We're in a rush, so if God wants to communicate something to us, then He had

CHAPTER TWO
Traits of a Disciple

Now when they saw the boldness of Peter and John, and perceived that they were uneducated and untrained men, they marveled. And they realized that they had been with Jesus. (Acts 4:13)

We need people today who walk and talk with Jesus Christ, people who, before they even speak a single word, give evidence that there is something different about them. We need people who, through their godly lifestyles, have earned the right to be heard. What we need today are people who have been with Jesus.

Let's say that you saw someone whose face was bright red. You might ask, "Were you in the sun recently?", because you see the evidence in that person's face. In the same way, people need to see the evidence of Christ in our lives. They should be able to tell that we have been with Him.

Could that be said of you? Could someone look at you and your lifestyle and say, "That person has been with Jesus"? Could people tell that you are a follower of Jesus Christ by the way you treat others? By the way you are around your family? By your outlook on life?

Abiding

As I pointed out in the previous chapter, the first result of discipleship is that you will bear fruit. But how? We find the answer in John 15:4, where Jesus says quite plainly that we must abide in Him: "Abide in Me, and I in you. As the branch cannot bear fruit of itself, unless it abides in the vine, neither can you, unless you abide in Me."

So what does it mean to abide? It is much the same as following Christ: walking with Him consistently as our Lord and our friend. But it takes the idea further. To abide means that we are sinking our roots deep into a love relationship with Jesus. It is not simply walking with and serving Him when it is easy, convenient, or popular. When we abide in Christ, we remain in fellowship with Him daily, regardless of outward circumstances or inner emotions.

In this verse, Jesus uses the analogy of a vine to describe the importance of abiding. It causes us to think of vegetation that draws its strength from the soil of the earth. If we were to uproot a tree and move it to another area, then after awhile uproot it again and move it to a different place, it's quite possible we would damage that tree. And if we repeated the process several more times, the tree would most certainly die. Yet that is how many Christians try to live.

Some believers have never found a place of consistency in their walk with God. Often they are the ones who respond again and again to invitations to receive Christ. They find themselves in a continual cycle of making "commitments" to Christ, but quickly fall away when they face the pressures and temptations of the real world.

Following his sin with Bathsheba, David said, "Create in me a clean heart, O God, and renew a steadfast spirit within me." (Ps. 51:10). A "steadfast" spirit could also be translated a "consistent" spirit. So to bear fruit, we must consistently sink our roots deeply into a relationship with Jesus Christ and walk with Him.

Real spiritual growth comes only through discipline and

perseverance. Unfortunately, we often substitute activity for fellowship with God. We see this in an account recorded in Luke 10, in which Martha and Mary had invited Jesus to their home for a meal. Martha desperately tried to prepare a feast fit for a king, literally, but she whipped herself into a frenzy in the process. We find Martha "distracted with much serving," while Mary, on the other hand, had set aside the cares of the world to sit at the feet of Jesus and drink in His every word. Mary is the picture of a disciple who has learned the importance of listening, while Martha is the picture of many Christians today.

In our chaotic world, we can easily identify with Martha as we often must choose between a certain activity and setting aside time to spend with God. And like Martha, when we fail to sit at the feet of Jesus, we usually end up frustrated.

There is no doubt that Martha's intentions were good; however, she substituted work for worship. There is a time to be active in serving God, but before we can effectively work for Him, we need to first learn to wait on Him. Before we can *give out* to others, we must *take in* for ourselves. Before we can disciple others, we must learn for ourselves what it means to be a disciple. A disciple will always take time to sit at the feet of Jesus.

This story takes on greater significance when you think of a disciple as a learner, as one who comes to be taught. More than a student passively listening to a lecture, this narrative conveys the idea that the one teaching possesses full knowledge, and the one listening is doing so intently, marking every inflection of the master's voice and holding an intense desire to apply what is learned.

The attitude of a real disciple would be similar to that of someone on a plane that is about to crash. That person would listen carefully and intently as the instructions were given on how to survive the crash, no doubt hanging on every word. If I were that person and the flight crew was telling me how to use a parachute, I would not be interested in the book I had brought along. I would listen intently because my life depended on it. That is how Mary listened to Jesus, and that is how we should listen as well.

God is far more interested in our inspiration than our perspiration. Mary learned the secret of abiding, and we need to learn it as well—if we truly want to be His disciples.

"They Had Been with Jesus"

In the Book of Acts, we find another story of two disciples, Peter and John, who had spent time with Jesus and had been radically impacted by their relationship with Him. As a result, they wanted to tell as many people as possible about it, which led to their being arrested and brought before the Sanhedrin.

It was a source of amazement to these religious leaders that ordinary fishermen were so well-versed in the Scriptures and, more importantly, in the understanding of them. They appeared to have more understanding in the Word of God than even the rabbis, the trained professionals. How was this so? Acts 4:13 provides the answer: "And they realized that they had been with Jesus" (NIV).

These two men were present on the Day of Pentecost, when the power of God had dramatically fallen. A sound like a mighty rushing wind had filled the room, and divided flames of fire rested upon each disciple as they had been waiting for this power from on high.

Pentecost was now over, and those little flames were no longer visible over the heads of the disciples, but they were replaced by burning hearts. So Peter and John, with hearts aflame, were headed over to the temple to pray one day. It was 3:00 PM on an ordinary day. We don't read of an angel instructing them to go to the temple because a miracle would be performed, nor do we read of a pillar of fire going before them and leading them to their destination. It was a day like any other day. They didn't know what God was about to do.

In the Books of Acts, we never read about a miracle being

announced ahead of time. They happened as God sovereig|
chose to perform them. Peter and John didn't put up posters
around town that read "Miracle service at the Beautiful Gate!
3:00 PM" They didn't have miracle ministries in the Book of Acts,
but they did have gospel-preaching and Bible-teaching ministries. They served God with the gifts He had given them, and God
sovereignly did the miracles when and where He wanted to do
them.

As Peter and John were making their way to the temple, they
passed by the Beautiful Gate where a lame man was sitting and
begging, probably a fixture outside the temple. He may have had
his friends carry him there and strategically position him to be
seen by people coming from a prayer service, whom he hoped
might give a little money to a man in need. I wonder if people
stopped noticing him after awhile. Maybe they even stepped over
him as they went on their way.

Sometimes we can do the same thing. We can be so indiffer-
ent to people around us, so oblivious to the pain they are experiencing. For the most part we are preoccupied, chatting away on
our cell phones, rushing here and there. As a result, we miss the
needs of people and miss opportunities right on our doorstep.

But on this day in Jerusalem, the supernatural invaded the
natural. God decided to shake things up a little. Simon Peter did
not, in and of himself, have the faith to do what he was about
to do. God had given Peter a special measure of faith, enabling
him to say to the man, "Silver and gold I do not have, but what I
do have I give you: In the name of Jesus Christ of Nazareth, rise
up and walk" (Acts 3:16). And Peter didn't stop there. He took
the man by his hand and helped him stand to his feet. This was
another a sink-or-swim moment for Peter. It would be either a
great victory or a horrible disaster. Peter was going for broke, as
he often did.

Once, as he watched Jesus walking on the water on the Sea of

Galilee, he said, "Lord, if it is You, command me to come to You on the water" (Matt. 14:28). A smile surely must have appeared on Jesus' face as He told Peter to come to Him. When Peter swung his legs over the side of the boat and slowly lowered himself onto the water, much to his amazement, it supported his full weight. He took one step . . . and then another . . . and another. . . . We don't know what broke Peter's concentration, but he apparently took his eyes off Jesus. Maybe he looked over his shoulder to see if the other disciples were watching him. Maybe he looked down at the waves surrounding him. Whatever it was, it caused him to falter. He began sinking and cried out, "Lord, save me!" So Jesus pulled him up.

We tend to focus on Peter's doubting when we read this story, but we should also commend him for the simple fact that he was the only one who walked on the water. If getting out of the boat had been the wrong thing for him to do, then Jesus never would have invited him to come. Peter clearly was willing to take steps of faith.

And here he was, about to take another one. As he pulled the lame man to his feet, "instantly the man's feet and ankles became strong. He jumped to his feet and began to walk. Then he went with them into the temple courts, walking and jumping, and praising God" (Acts 3:7–8). As people began to realize what had happened, that this had been the same man who sat begging by the Beautiful Gate, they began to gather around the three men. God then showed Peter that he was to preach the gospel, so Peter gave an excellent presentation of who Jesus Christ is.

This, however, didn't play well with everyone in the temple. The Sadducees (the religious leaders who did not believe in the resurrection of the dead) had the temple police apprehend Peter and John and throw them in jail. The next day, the two were brought before the Sanhedrin, which included Annas and Caiaphas, both culpable in the crucifixion of Jesus. They had probably concluded that once Jesus was dead, their problem was over.

But ironically, here were Peter and John. They thought they had destroyed the Christian faith by killing Christ, yet what they did not understand was they had played into the plan and purpose of God. Jesus was living in each of His followers.

This story, among other things, shows us how God can use ordinary people in extraordinary ways. It is important for us to understand, however, that the miracles we read about in Acts did not necessarily happen every day. Acts was written over a thirty-year period. Most days were like yours and mine. These Christians would get up every morning and walk by faith, allowing God to lead them. And for disciples like Peter and John, people took note that they had been with Jesus.

Four Marks of an Effective Disciple

Have you been with Jesus? These four elements working in the lives of the disciples caused them to turn their world upside down.

1. A person who has been with Jesus will boldly share his or her faith. Just months earlier, this same Peter had denied Jesus and was ashamed of Him. Now he was seemingly fearless, speaking with the same boldness that Jesus himself spoke with. When you spend time with Jesus, you will become more like Him.

Sometimes when couples have been married for a long time, they can begin taking on one another's traits. They can finish each other's sentences. They know how their spouse will react to this or to that. My wife and I have often joked that between the two of us, we have one complete brain. When you are around someone a lot, you become more and more like them.

God's objective in the life of the believer is to make us into the image of Jesus Christ. He wants you to become more and more like Him each and every day. Romans 8:29 says, "For God knew his people in advance, and he chose them to become like his Son, so that his Son would be the firstborn among many brothers and sisters" (NLT).

name Christian is not one that the followers of Jesus came up with. It was a description given to them by their critics, because it meant they were like Jesus. A literal translation would be, "They were of the party of Christ." Are you in the party of Christ? Or are you ashamed to be identified with Jesus? The religious leaders of the first century realized there was no stopping the Christians, because they had been with Jesus. Can people recognize that about you?

2. A person who has been with Jesus will know Scripture. One thing that arrested the Sanhedrin's attention was Peter's grasp and knowledge of Scripture. As you read through his sermon (see Acts 3:11–26; 4:8–13), note the number of times he quotes from various passages. It shows us that when you have been with Jesus, you will spend time in His Word. The Bible is the autobiography of God. It tells you everything you need to know about God, about life, and about yourself. It tells you how to live, what to do, and what not to do. It tells you how to think, how to act, and how to react. If you want to get closer to God, you have to study the Bible, because Jesus said, "Behold, I have come—in the volume of the book it is written of Me—to do Your will, O God" (Heb. 10:7).

You can read the writings or biographies of certain people to learn about them, but God has given us His book, the Bible, so we can learn about Him.

3. A person who has been with Jesus will be a person of prayer. After being released and told to no longer preach their message, Peter and John joined the other disciples. And what did they do? They held a prayer meeting (see Acts 4:29), which gave them even more boldness.

4. A person who has been with Jesus will be persecuted. Peter and John were arrested. And because we have been with Jesus, we will be, in effect, like Jesus and treated the same as Jesus. If everyone likes you, if everyone thinks you are wonderful, if you don't have an enemy anywhere, then something is wrong with you.

Maybe you have thought the opposite, that if you are a Christian, then you should be sweetness and light and that everyone should love you. There is some truth to that. You should be a loving person and a sweet person and a kind person. But you also have to be a godly person and a truthful person and a righteous person. And if you are, that will bother some people. You can tell a lot about a person by who their enemies and friends are. If you are really walking with Jesus, then you will face persecution. And if you are a true believer, then persecution will not weaken you, but only strengthen you. If you are not a true believer, then you will abandon what little faith you have.

Then again, sometimes we are persecuted because we are obnoxious and unnecessarily offensive. We behave like self-righteous, insensitive fools, and then wonder why people don't like us. We console ourselves with the thought that we are blessed because we have been persecuted, when all along we were persecuted for behaving like idiots and because we don't know how to love people or be compassionate. The gospel has enough built-in offense. Let's not make it worse. Let's deliver it with compassion.

Jesus said, "Blessed are those who are persecuted for righteousness' sake, for theirs is the kingdom of heaven." (Matt. 5:10). May the persecution you face be a result of your representing Christ, or more to the point, because you are like Christ. That is the right reason to be persecuted.

The Christian life is tough at times. But if, for you, it is all about feeling good and having everything go your way, then you won't like being a disciple. Being a follower of Christ is the most joyful life there is. It is the most exciting life there is. It is the most challenging life there is. But it also is a life in which you are under the command of someone other than yourself.

Just as soldiers receive and carry out orders from their commanding officer, we must respond to the orders of our commander-in-chief, Jesus Christ. The Bible says, "You therefore must endure hardship as a good soldier of Jesus Christ" (2 Tim. 2:3). Soldiers have made a commitment to serve and protect their country, so they respond to the orders they are given. They don't argue with their commanding officer. In the same way, disciples have made a commitment to serve Jesus Christ. They need to be willing to respond to Him when He leads them. They do what He tells them to do. They go where He tells them to go. They say what He wants them to say. And more and more, they become like Him until the day they see Him face to face. So if you don't want to live that way, if it all has to be about you, then you will not make it as a disciple, and you will be missing out.

Have you been with Jesus? Today as you come into contact with people, I hope they will able to tell that you have. I hope there is an intangible something about the way you act, the way you speak, and the way you are that prompts them to wonder what it is it about you.

While there is of course a place for words in preaching the gospel, it is also a glorious thing when we earn the right to be heard by the way that we live, when someone says, "There is something special about you. There is something different about you, and I want to know more about what you believe. Please tell me."

You never know what opportunities will open up for you each day. That is why every Christian needs to always be ready to respond to the leading of the Lord, just as Peter did. We are told in Scripture, "Be ready in season and out of season . . . " (2 Tim. 4:2). Or, as another translation puts it, "Be prepared, whether the time is favorable or not" (NLT).

May God help us to be like the first-century believers and turn our world upside down in the midst of persecution, challenges, and temptation. May people be able to tell that we have been with Jesus.

CHAPTER THREE
The Cost of Discipleship

And being in Bethany at the house of Simon the leper, as He sat at the table, a woman came having an alabaster flask of very costly oil of spikenard. Then she broke the flask and poured it on His head. (Mark 14:3)

One of the reasons the Christians of the first century turned their world upside down in such a dramatic way was their sense of abandon. God would say to Peter, "Reach down, take that lame man's hand, and pull him to his feet," and he would do it. God would tell Philip, "Go to the desert," and he would go (see Acts 8:26–27). They were willing to take risks.

In committing to be a disciple, one of the factors you must consider is the cost. Obedience to God's plan of discipleship definitely will be costly. Too often, a would-be disciple desires God's best, but fails to pay the price to attain it. How can we be willing to give so little to the One who gave so much for us? He gave everything to us and He expects nothing less in return.

Yet many believers are like the farmer who was known for his stinginess. When his cow gave birth to two calves, he looked at them and said, "Lord, I'm so thankful for this blessing that I'm going to give You one of my calves." He proudly told his wife of his decision, which surprised her in light of his normally selfish ways.

When she asked him which calf he was planning to give to

the Lord, he replied, "I'm not sure yet."

Time went by, and one of the calves began to get sick. A few days later, the farmer came out of the barn, the lifeless calf draped over his arms, and sorrowfully announced, "Honey, I've got bad news. The Lord's calf just died."

Likewise, some Christians give God what they no longer want. But that is not the attitude we should have. How we miss out! How we misunderstand! God doesn't want our leftovers. He deserves the best. He has given so much to us that we should want to give everything we have back to Him.

"She Did What She Could"

We see this modeled by Mary—the same Mary who sat at the feet of Jesus while Martha hurried to prepare a meal for Him. Later, in another account, we find her offering Jesus the most precious thing she probably owned. In fact, she did something so outstanding, so significant, that Jesus said, "Assuredly, I say to you, wherever this gospel is preached in the whole world, what this woman has done will also be told as a memorial to her" (Mark 14:9).

By this time in the life and ministry of Jesus, He had already had a number of confrontational exchanges with the religious leaders. They wanted Him dead, plain and simple. The problem was that Jerusalem was overflowing with pilgrims who had arrived for the Passover celebration. Jesus still had His admirers, and the religious leaders were afraid that if they were to arrest and kill Him, they would have a revolt on their hands.

So while the forces of darkness were amassing to do their wicked work, Jesus decided to share a meal with friends and followers at the house of Simon the leper. Presumably this was Simon the *healed* leper. Lazarus was there, who had been resurrected from the dead. His sisters Martha and Mary were present, as were the other apostles. I would have loved to eavesdrop on the conversations that took place in that home. Jesus had just delivered the Olivet Discourse, which was His overview of Last Days events. Maybe there were some follow-up questions on that. Or perhaps someone turned to Lazarus and said, "What was it like to die and come back again? Tell us more."

At some point during this visit with Jesus, Mary did something unexpected and very unusual. She took some special and costly perfume, broke open the flask, and poured it on the head of Jesus. The perfume was called spikenard, and presumably it would have been imported from India. Most likely it was a family heirloom and worth a lot of money. It would have been one thing to sprinkle a few drops on Him, which was culturally acceptable at that time. But Mary wanted to do something outstanding, something significant and even extravagant to show her deep love for Him, so she poured the whole bottle on Jesus.

However, not everyone appreciated her sacrifice: "Some of those present were saying indignantly to one another, 'Why this waste of perfume? It could have been sold for more than a year's wages and the money given to the poor.' And they rebuked her harshly" (John 14:4–5 NIV). In other words, was such an extravagant gesture really necessary? Was that an act of good stewardship? Was that the right thing to do?

This is typical of so many people today. Like dutiful Pharisees, they will give only what is required by God. They want to get by on the bare minimum. They will ask questions like, "Can I do this and still be a Christian?" In essence, they are wondering what is the bare minimum they can give to God. Sure, they will pray briefly before a meal or before going to sleep—if they remember to. They will read the Bible—if they can make time in their busy schedule for it. They will give something to the Lord—if they have a little spare change in their pocket. They will sing the worship songs in church—as long as the worship leaders don't get carried away.

So what was the inspiration behind this sense of abandon and sacrifice in Mary? It was Jesus himself. Her idea was that nothing is too good for the Lord. And what could be wrong with that?

Jesus both defended and commended Mary for her sacrificial act: "Why are you bothering her? She has done a beautiful thing to me. The poor you will always have with you, and you can help them any time you want. But you will not always have me. She did what she could. She poured perfume on my body beforehand to prepare for my burial" (Mark 14:6–8 NIV).

Mary did what she could because she understood that Jesus would do what He did. If we, like Mary, know anything of what God has done for us, then we will want to do more for Him. Nothing is ever wasted when it is done from a right motive for the glory of God. You can't do everything, but you can do something. You can't win all of the people in the world to Christ, but you can win some. So do what you can. We all have something that we can do. And we must all do what we can while we can. Shouldn't we give Him the finest that we have to offer? Doesn't Jesus deserve our best?

One day your life will come to an end. And you can be assured you will not regret going to church too much. You will not regret reading the Bible too much. You will not regret sharing your faith. What you will regret is that you didn't do these things more.

Selling Out for So Little

The Bible makes it clear that we are not our own. We have been bought with a price, and therefore we are to glorify God with everything we are (see 1 Cor. 6:19–20). We must recognize that we belong to Him, that our time is His time, that our life is His life, and that our resources and possessions are His resources and possessions. We must consider all of this when we are committing to discipleship.

I heard about a remarkable method hunters in Africa have used to catch monkeys. They take a coconut and cut a little hole large enough for a monkey to reach into, but not large enough for it to pull its fist out. Next, they hollow out the coconut, put some warm rice inside, and place them under trees where their nets are hanging. Then the hunters wait.

When the monkeys smell the rice, they reach inside the coconuts. But the hunters have learned that the monkeys will not open their fist to let go of the rice, and therefore cannot get the coconut off. When the monkeys start banging the coconuts on the ground in frustration, the hunters arrive and easily capture them. Even as the monkeys see the nets, they still won't let go of the coconuts, because they want the rice. As a result, they are trapped.

Many people live their whole lives for their handful of rice: a handful of possessions . . . a handful of pursuits . . . a handful of pleasures. They give up what God could do in their lives in exchange for fleeting, temporal things. Like Esau, they sell everything for a bowl of stew (see Gen. 25:29–34).

True discipleship takes sacrifice. In Luke 9 we find a passage that illustrates the extent of a disciple's commitment:

> Now it happened as they journeyed on the road, that someone said to Him, "Lord, I will follow You wherever You go."
>
> And Jesus said to him, "Foxes have holes and birds of the air have nests, but the Son of Man has nowhere to lay His head." (vv. 57–58)

In modern language, Jesus was saying, "Look, buddy, I'm not headed to the Jerusalem Ritz-Carlton. You might want to reconsider. Mine is a life of difficulty and sacrifice. Do you know where I'm going? Ultimately I'm going to die on the cross. Is that where you want to go? Consider what you're saying!"

We must give this man some credit, though. He was inspired. He saw Jesus, admired Him, and immediately blurted out that he wanted to follow Him. He seemed to have a good heart, but he was impulsive. He had not first counted the cost. He did not know what was ahead. Jesus was making it clear that if this man was to be a disciple, then he would have to forsake all that he had. It is not any different for us. We must have the same attitude of detachment to anyone or anything that would prevent us from fully following Him.

A few verses later, Jesus states, "No one, having put his hand to the plow, and looking back, is fit for the kingdom of God" (v. 62). That is a stern warning for those who wish to live a life of second guessing.

In another passage, Jesus used a military analogy to illustrate this concept:

> "Or suppose a king is about to go to war against another king. Will he not first sit down and consider whether he is able with ten thousand men to oppose the one coming against him with twenty thousand? If he is not able, he will send a delegation while the other is still a long way off and will ask for terms of peace. (Luke 14:31–32 NIV)

Jesus was not necessarily implying that the king had only ten thousand troops available. It's quite possible that the king had fifty thousand troops, but was only willing to commit ten thousand for battle.

In other words, Jesus would say to anyone who is considering discipleship, "I'm not asking whether you are willing to commit 10 percent or 20 percent, or even 50 percent to Me. If you are not willing to commit everything to Me and recognize My absolute right over everything in your life, then you cannot be My disciple."

What (or Who) Is Holding You Back?

Discipleship not only requires *giving* our best, but it also requires *giving up* anything that would hinder us in our commitment to follow

Christ. Hebrews 12:1–2 tells us,

> Therefore, since we are surrounded by such a great cloud
> of witnesses, let us throw off everything that hinders and
> the sin that so easily entangles, and let us run with perse-
> verance the race marked out for us. Let us fix our eyes on
> Jesus, the author and perfecter of our faith, who for the joy
> set before him endured the cross, scorning its shame, and
> sat down at the right hand of the throne of God. (NIV)

As we seek to walk with Christ, we can sometimes travel with
too much weight. We drag things along that should not be in our
lives. It might be something we are doing that is slowing us down,
or it might be someone we are spending time with. But we need
to get rid of excess weight.

Whenever my friend Franklin Graham visits, he wants to
go for a run. He will say, "Come on, Greg. Let's go for a run in the
morning!"

"OK," I say. "Looking forward to that."

Franklin is a good runner. He is disciplined. He can run consistently for a good forty-five minutes, sometimes nearly an hour. I, on
the other hand, am good for about four minutes. Then I am tired. So
we will start running. As I start to slow down, Franklin will say, "Greg,
come on! Greg! Greg, run!" So I will run a little bit more.

"I am just going to walk," I will tell him after awhile.

"Come on! Run!" he says.

"I am running," I tell him. "In my heart I am running with you."

I think Franklin realizes that I slow him down. He is trying to
run a race, and I am impeding his performance.

We have people in our lives that can have the same effect on
us spiritually. When we are around them, they slow us down,
because they don't have the same interest in the things of God.

We'll say, "Hey, let's go to church today!"

"Oh, I don't know. It's raining. It is so dangerous with the rain.

Do you want to go to the mall instead?"

They drag us down, and we know it.

The Bible tells the story of Abraham and his nephew, Lot. Lot was not committed to walking with God like his uncle was. And whenever Lot was around, he seemed to drag Abraham down. God even told Abraham to part company with Lot, but he refused for a time. Yet it wasn't until Abraham unloaded Lot that God began to speak to him and bless him again, because Lot was slowing him down.

We all know people like that who slow us down spiritually. That is why Paul advised Timothy, "Run from anything that stimulates youthful lusts. Instead, pursue righteous living, faithfulness, love, and peace. Enjoy the companionship of those who call on the Lord with pure hearts" (2 Tim. 2:22 NLT). Spend time with people who have the same commitment to discipleship as you do—not those who will drag you down.

Understand the Terms

To count the cost is to understand the terms of the commitment. How much are you willing to give?

In our pursuit to become disciples, we make decisions every day that will either encourage or discourage our spiritual growth. When we get up in the morning, it's either the news or the Bible. On the weekend, it's either sleeping in or going to church. In dealing with others, it's either harboring a grudge or choosing to forgive. When thinking about the future, it's either worrying or praying. With each choice, we either will progress or regress, advance or retreat in our quest to be His disciples.

If you look back at this point in your life and have a number of regrets, you can't change that. But you can change what you do today and what you will do tomorrow. You can change your course if need be.

Is your commitment to discipleship like that of the farmer

who determined it was "the Lord's calf" that had died? Or, are you willing to pay the price and commit to radical Christian living?

Every hour, every minute you have given to serve Jesus, every resource you have invested, and every thought you have given over to His Word are not wasted. They are the best possible investments.

CHAPTER FOUR

Discipleship and the Bible

Then Jesus said to those Jews who believed Him, "If you abide in My word, you are My disciples indeed." (John 8:31)

I t always amazes me to see how much care and cultivation it takes to make flowers grow. My wife loves to plant flowers. She can spend hours pulling weeds, driving out snails, and amending the soil. It is necessary for their growth. Yet how quickly and easily weeds can sprout up and take over. It seems a weed can bloom in the middle of a street or a crack in the sidewalk, and without any caretaker or special watering, it does just fine. But the delicate, vulnerable flowers require constant attention.

This is a classic illustration of the contrast between a believer's new nature and old nature. If we want to be closer to Christ and live a life that is pleasing to Him, we need to cultivate and nurture our new nature. The moment we stop strengthening and building up the new nature, the moment the old one comes back to haunt us—just like a weed growing in the street. It takes very little encouragement for our old nature to cause us trouble. All we need to do is neglect the new nature. As the apostle Paul wrote, "I say then: Walk in the Spirit, and you shall not fulfill the lust of the flesh" (Gal. 5:16). There are disciplines every believer must maintain if he wants to live the Christian life as it was meant to be lived.

The Key to Spiritual Progress

In this chapter, we'll examine the first of these disciplines, found in John 8:31, where Jesus said, "If you abide in My word, you are My disciples indeed." If you and I want to truly be disciples of Jesus Christ, then we must continue to abide in the Word of God.

To a great measure, success or failure in the Christian life depends on how much of God's Word we get into our hearts and minds on a regular basis and how obedient we are to it. Everything we need to know about God is taught in the Bible. If we neglect the study of Scripture, then our spiritual life will ultimately fall into disrepair.

President Abraham Lincoln once said of the Bible, "It is the best gift which God has ever given man. All the good from the Savior of the world is communicated to us through this Book. But for that Book we could not know right from wrong. All those things desirable to man are contained in it."[2] Honest Abe was exactly right.

The Bible is the most amazing document ever given to man. Technically speaking, it is not one book, but sixty-six books written over a 1,600-year period of time by everyone from kings to peasants, from philosophers to fishermen, and from poets to statesmen. Each of them were inspired by God to write down His Word. They were not the authors; God was. He breathed each word.

Why is it, then, that so many believers fail to open their Bibles? Could it be that many Christians simply lack that spiritual hunger for the truth? One way for a doctor to know whether a person is healthy is to check his or her appetite. When there isn't any appetite, it usually means something is wrong. In the same way, some Christians don't have an appetite for the Word of God. Some see reading God's Word as a duty, a bit of drudgery, an obligation. But that can change when they see the difference it makes in their daily lives.

Hungry Christians are healthy Christians. The Bible tells us, "As newborn babes, desire the pure milk of the word, that you may grow thereby, if indeed you have tasted that the Lord is gracious" (1 Pet. 2:2–3). To desire the pure milk of the Word means that we intensely long for the teaching of the Bible because we want to grow. If we are not making progress spiritually, then it is very possible that we are not yearning for the Scripture.

The prophet Hosea's cry is still relevant: "My people are destroyed for lack of knowledge" (Hos. 4:6). Today, many believers throw in the towel, fall into sin, or are misled by false teachings because they have never developed the vital discipline of studying the Bible on a regular basis. If we are to be disciples of Jesus Christ, leading effective and successful Christian lives, then God's Word must be a priority.

Proverbs 2:1–9 provides a wonderful series of promises that will help us get the most from our study of Scripture. For every promise, there is a condition that we must fulfill. The conditions listed in the first five verses state that we must receive His words and treasure His commandments, cry out for discernment, and seek understanding as though we were mining for gold.

Know for Yourself

Let's examine the first of these principles for getting the most out of Scripture, which we find in verse 1: "My son, if you receive my words, and treasure my commands within you. . . ." To get the most out of Scripture, we must receive it and treasure it.

Referring to the Christians in Berea, Acts 17:11 says, "Now the Bereans were of more noble character than the Thessalonians, for they received the message with great eagerness and examined the Scriptures every day to see if what Paul said was true" (NIV). The Bereans checked the accuracy of Paul's teaching against Scripture. If they examined the apostle's teaching, then how much more should we be checking out our own pastors, teachers, and so-called modern apostles and prophets?

Some people today claim to speak for God, but if anyone questions the validity of what they say, such a person is rebuked for daring to challenge those who claim to be modern apostles or prophets. What foolishness! No one is above being questioned. If the apostle Paul was scrutinized according to Scripture, then how much more should be those who often contradict it.

Together with a search of Scripture, the Bereans received the message with "all readiness of mind" (KJV). This was not simply eagerness on the part of these believers to learn something new, but a willingness to reinforce and apply what they already knew.

Many Christians think they know more than they actually do. Often apparently mature believers are reduced to a blank stare when faced with a question concerning a basic Bible doctrine. They know what they are supposed to believe, but they are unable to defend it biblically. They believe something only because they have been told it is true.

This is very dangerous. We should never hinge our faith merely on what someone has said to us, no matter how credible and godly the source. If that person is saying something that is incorrect, our faith could be shattered. This is why we must base our faith solely on God's Word. We need to know it for ourselves.

How to Study

The Bible tells us to "be diligent to present yourself approved to God, a worker who does not need to be ashamed, rightly dividing the word of truth" (2 Tim. 2:15). The phrase "rightly dividing" means "dissecting correctly, cutting straight" the word of truth.

Do you believe that Jesus Christ is God? That is an essential doctrine. Do you believe that Jesus Christ is the only way to the Father? Do you believe that God has a plan for your life and wants to reveal His will for you? If so, can you back your beliefs biblically? Unfortunately, many Christians can't answer these questions with intelligent, scriptural responses.

One reason for this is that often we do not read the Bible intelligently. Many times we read, but we fail to understand what is being said in its context. We have no idea who is speaking and what the circumstances are surrounding the passage.

For instance, reading in the Old Testament about various animal sacrifices could be very confusing if I did not have a basic understanding of the New Testament. I might conclude that the best way to approach God is to sacrifice an animal. With an understanding of the New Testament, however, I realize that the sacrificial system was foreshadowing what Jesus would do on the cross.

Here are some key questions you might ask yourself as you open the Bible and study a passage of Scripture:

- What is the main subject of the passage?
- Who are the people revealed in this passage?
- Who is speaking?
- About whom is the passage speaking?
- What is the key verse?
- What does it teach me about Jesus?

As you read, it is also very important to ask how the text might apply to your daily living. When reading a passage, ask yourself these questions:

- Is there a sin mentioned that I need to confess or forsake?
- Is there a command given that I should obey?
- Is there a promise made that I can look to in my current circumstances?
- Is there a prayer given that I could pray?

As you read, stop and think about what God may be showing you. It's good to chew your spiritual food. That is what is meant by meditating on Scripture. We are better off reading five verses slowly and understanding what they mean than reading five chapters quickly and not getting anything out of them. Learn to slow down. Learn to allow the Holy Spirit to speak to you through each passage as you read.

Psalm 1 gives us an example of a person who has learned to walk with God and tells us that "his delight is in the law of the Lord, and on his law he meditates day and night" (v. 1 NIV). As disciples, we should do the same.

This brings us to another important ingredient in learning from Scripture, which we find in Proverbs 2:3: "Cry out for insight, and ask for understanding" (NLT). To get the most out of Bible study, we need to pray for understanding. We need to come before the Lord and pray something like,

> "Father, I believe You are the author of this Book. I believe, as You say in Scripture, that all Scripture is breathed by You. Therefore I am asking You, as the author, to take me on a guided tour. Help me to understand, and show me how these truths apply to my life."

That form of sincere prayer will cause the Bible to come alive in your time of study.

The Bible tells us if we want to know God, then we should seek Him and His wisdom as though we were "mining for gold" or searching for treasures (see Prov. 2:4).

As believers in the United States, I doubt that we recognize what a treasure the Bible is to us. Recently, I was talking with a Bible publisher who told me there is a growing trend today in which consumers are more interested in how a Bible coordinates with their outfit than the type of study features and helps it may contain. We have been spoiled in many ways. Many of us have more than one Bible at home. I own Bibles in different sizes, shapes, and translations.

But in China and other countries where the Bible is restricted, even prohibited, it is a treasure. I've heard stories of believers who have had only one Bible for an entire congregation. They take that Bible, tear out pages, and give them to individual members of the congregation to memorize. For many of these Christians, Bibles are as valuable as gold—even more so. We need to see that same value in God's Word and not take it for granted. As Psalm 19:9–10 says, "The laws of the Lord are true; each one is fair. They are more desirable than gold, even the finest gold" (NLT).

When you are reading through the Bible, think about it as though you were mining for gold. Have you ever dropped a quarter? Do you look for a quarter if you drop it? I do. Do you look for a dime? I do. Do you look for a penny? I do, depending on the circumstances.

Let's say that you somehow misplaced one million dollars. Do you think you would go searching for it? I think I would. If I am willing to look for a quarter, then I definitely would look for a million dollars.

There is buried gold in the pages of Scripture. You need to get to it, search for it, and find what is there in the Bible for you.

Why Memorize?

The best way for me to remember things is to write them down. When I write something down, it is engraved more deeply into my memory, much deeper than if I had only read it. I might not even have to refer to what I wrote. Writing something down seems to help the material enter my mind and gives it more staying power. It is a good practice to keep a journal or notebook with your Bible. When you study the Scripture personally and a passage speaks to you, write down what God has shown you. Maybe it won't be useful right at that moment, but the next day, or even a month later, it may be just what you need.

Once Scripture is ingrained in your memory, it always will be there to use. There will be times when that verse or passage you memorized will pay great dividends. It will bring comfort to your heart, as well as needed strength in a time of intense temptation. The psalmist wrote, "Your word I have hidden in my heart, that I might not sin against You" (Ps. 119:11). Although it is good to carry a Bible in your briefcase, backpack, or purse, the best place to carry it is in your heart.

God tells us, "Fix these words of mine in your hearts and minds; tie them as symbols on your hands and bind them on your foreheads. Teach them to your children, talking about them when you sit at home and when you walk along the road, when you lie down and when you get up" (Deut. 11:18–19 NIV).

Colossians 3:16 says, "Let the word of Christ dwell in you richly . . ." (NIV). That could be translated, "Let the word of Christ permeate your life," or, "Let the word of Christ be at home inside of you." In other words, let the Bible fill your life. Fall in love with the Word of God. You will never regret it.

What you will regret is all the time you spent watching television. You will regret all the time you spent surfing the Web. But you never will regret a single minute you spent studying the Bible or memorizing it.

Have you ever felt bad after you have gone to church? *Another couple of wasted hours at church. What a drag. We could have been home watching another mindless television program. We could have gone to another bad movie.* I have never felt like I wasted time when I have spent it worshiping God and studying His Word.

Applying What We Learn

It is not enough to study the Bible on a daily basis or even memorize it; it must affect the way we live.

It is not enough to go through the Word of God; the Word of God must go through us.

It is not how we mark our Bibles; it is how our Bible marks us.

Ultimately we must apply what we learn from the Bible to our everyday actions and activities. Remember, Jesus said that if we continue in His Word, then we are His disciples (see John 8:31). The word "continue" is the same word Jesus used in John 15:7 when He spoke of "abiding." He said, "If you abide in Me, and My words abide in you, you will ask what you desire, and it shall be done for you."

We abide in Jesus as we draw strength and resources from Him. In the same way that a vine draws its resources from the soil and the branch draws its resources from the vine, we are to maintain unbroken fellowship, communion, and friendship with God. If we are abiding in God's Word, it means we are drawing our ideas and lifestyle from it. Consequently, our actions and speech are being affected.

Is God's Word affecting you today? Is it sustaining your life? Is it controlling your thoughts, the way you conduct your business, your home life, and even your free time? If not, then you are not a disciple. It is only when we put ourselves under the authority of His Word and submit to its teaching that we become disciples.

Which Type of Hearer Are You?

In Luke 8 we find a story called the Parable of the Sower, which illustrates the common obstacles to God's Word taking root in our lives. The seed represents God's Word, while the soil represents the different types of people who receive God's Word.

The first mentioned in this story is what I call the *highway hearer*: "A sower went out to sow his seed. And as he sowed, some fell by the wayside; and it was trampled down, and the birds of the air devoured it" (v. 5). The seed never takes root with highway hearers. They hear God's Word, but they simply don't believe it. It is not as though they embrace it or say they want to believe. They are just not interested. They are not open-minded, and they are not seekers.

Next is the *rocky road hearer*: "Some [seeds] fell on rock; and as soon as it sprang up, it withered away because it lacked moisture" (v. 6). In contrast to the indifference of the highway hearers, the rocky road hearers embrace the message. They say, "Yes! This is it! This is what I have been searching for!" But a week later or maybe a month or two later, they just walk away from it. They say, "I am not into that anymore." They couldn't maintain enough longevity in their walk with God to bear any fruit. And time will tell whether they ever were truly converted to begin with.

This brings us to the *thorny hearer*: "And some [seeds] fell among thorns, and the thorns sprang up with it and choked it" (v. 7). This third type of hearer represents a gradual process that could last months, even a few years. Just as a weed doesn't burst out of the ground, grab a plant, and shake it violently, it is a gradual process that chokes out this particular kind of spiritual growth. It starts out with subtle things, like going to church less often and reading the Bible less. Spiritual priorities move down while other priorities move up—until all growth comes to a standstill.

Last, we have the *fruitful hearer*. "But others [seeds] fell on good ground, sprang up, and yielded a crop a hundredfold."

Why does this person bring forth fruit? Because he or she wants to. Good ground is made that way by the work of the Master Gardener and our cooperation. You don't naturally have a receptive heart. You make it receptive. Stumps need to be uprooted. Weeds must be pulled and burned so the new seed can be planted.

God has to work in the soil of the human heart. We don't like it when He comes along and removes something that we have allowed to be rooted in our lives, such as a boulder of sin or a weed of rebellion or a stump of disobedience. God says, "We have to get this stuff out of here so we have fertile and receptive soil for the seed of the Word of God, and then the fruit will grow."

God wants the seeds of His Word to permeate every area of your life—your home, your business, and your leisure time as well as your prayer time. Continuing in God's Word is a necessity for all who want to be His disciples.

CHAPTER FIVE

Discipleship and Prayer

Once Jesus was in a certain place praying. As he finished, one of his disciples came to him and said, "Lord, teach us to pray, just as John taught his disciples." (Luke 11:1 NLT)

Prayer should be second nature to a Christian, almost like breathing. But sadly, prayer is greatly lacking in the lives of many believers.

A disciple must be a person of prayer. Prayer is one of the essentials of discipleship. It is the key to having passion and power in our witness for Jesus Christ.

When Job encountered his many trials, he cried out, "If only there were someone to arbitrate between us, to lay his hand upon us both" (Job 9:33 NIV). Job couldn't find anyone to reason or argue for him, no one who would stand in the gap for him before God. He felt as though he couldn't get through to God.

Perhaps there have been times when you have felt this way. Maybe it seemed as though God wasn't really listening. But if you have received Jesus Christ as your Lord and Savior, this simply should not be the case, because Jesus has opened the way for us to stand boldly at the throne of grace to find help in time of need (see Heb. 4:16). The Bible tells us that Jesus lives to make intercession for us (see Heb. 7:25). Today we can approach God through Jesus, our Mediator: "For there is one God and one mediator between God and men, the man Christ Jesus" (1 Tim. 2:5 NIV).

The value of prayer is that it keeps us in touch with God. God wants you to get to know Him through prayer. He wants to reveal himself to you through prayer. We might expect God to give us all that we need for every situation all at once. That is not the way it is. In fact, that would be dangerous.

God has a lot to give us, but He gives it to us as we need it. Prayer brings us into dependence on God as He works in our lives.

In Matthew 6, we find Jesus dealing with several common misconceptions people have regarding prayer. The first misconception concerned motives. Jesus said, "And when you pray, do not be like the hypocrites, for they love to pray standing in the synagogues and on the street corners to be seen by men. I tell you the truth, they have received their reward in full . . ." (v. 5 NIV).

The problem with the religious people of that day, the Pharisees, was that they prayed to impress others. They could be seen on street corners and in the marketplace lifting up their hands and praying in a very ostentatious manner. Others would walk by and think, *Just look at that man of God. He loves God so much that he can't even wait to get to the synagogue to pray!*

What they didn't realize was that the person praying was most likely thinking, *What a man of God I am. Everyone is looking at me. Everyone is impressed with my spirituality. I am so holy.*

That type of attitude will result in a prayer left unheard by God. A person so concerned with what others are thinking about him is too full of himself to be effective in his prayer. He is like the self-righteous Pharisee Jesus mentioned who "prayed thus with himself" (Luke 18:11). God won't hear the prayer of a pride-filled person, because it is nothing less than sin. The Bible tells us that if we regard iniquity in our hearts, the Lord will not hear us (see Ps. 66:18). Make no mistake—spiritual pride is as much a sin as lying or immorality, even though it is a more subtle one.

The next misconception Jesus addressed was *how* the Pharisees were praying: "And when you pray, do not keep on babbling like pagans, for they think they will be heard because of their many words" (v. 7 NIV). The Pharisees were caught up in repeating ritualized prayers over and over again. They seemed to believe that the longer the prayer, the more spiritual and pleasing to God it was.

But God is not interested in eloquence. Prayer should come from the heart. He is not interested in how perfectly our prayers sound, or whether they rhyme, or how long they are. He is concerned with how genuine they are. One of the most eloquent prayers found in Scripture comes from a man who said, "God be merciful to me a sinner!" (Luke 18:13). Now that is an effective prayer. That is a man who was honest with God. He said what he was thinking and simply laid it out before the Lord. Sometimes we get so concerned with technique that we completely miss the whole point of prayer.

When Jesus used the word "pray," He used a word that literally means to "wish forward." To "wish" describes a desire, a hope of our heart. "Forward" implies action. It is the idea of wishing something from the depth of the heart and bringing that desire forward to the throne of God. Often our mouths and minds can go through some ritualized prayer, while our hearts never engage at all.

Sometimes people wonder what the best posture for prayer is. Is it on your knees? Is it OK to pray with your eyes open? You can pray with your eyes open. It is not a sin; it doesn't cancel out your prayer if your eyes are open. But I think it is a good thing to close your eyes when you pray, because it helps you to concentrate. Or, you can pray with your eyes closed. Also, you can pray on your knees, or you can pray sitting down or lying down. You can even pray while you are driving, but just be sure to keep your eyes open.

The Bible tells us that people prayed in all sorts of unusual places. They prayed in prison. They prayed on mountaintops. They prayed in valleys. One man even prayed from the belly of a whale, and God heard his prayer. Wherever you are, you can pray.

Another common misconception Jesus unmasked was the true purpose of prayer. He said, "Your Father knows what you need before you ask him" (v. 8 NIV). God knows our needs before we ask. Therefore, prayer is not instructing or informing God. Nor is it bending the will of God. Some people think they can influence God or move God a certain way through prayer. But nothing could be further from the truth. True prayer is not overcoming or changing God's reluctance; it's laying hold of His willingness. Prayer is not getting our will in heaven; it's getting God's will on earth. Martin Luther said, "By our praying . . . we are instructing ourselves more than Him."[3]

"Teach us to pray"

"Lord, teach us to pray. . . ." That was the request one of the disciples brought before Jesus. No doubt it was because the disciples had watched Jesus in prayer. Sometimes Jesus would stay up all night in the presence of His Heavenly Father and pray. While the disciples would be sleeping, Jesus would be praying. In the Garden of Gethsemane, shortly before His arrest, He told Peter, "Watch and pray, lest you enter into temptation. The spirit indeed is willing, but the flesh is weak" (Matt. 26:41).

In response to the disciple's request, Jesus gave us a template for prayer that we call The Lord's Prayer. A more accurate name for it would be The Disciples' Prayer, because it is for us to pray and not for Him to pray. Jesus never needed to pray, "And forgive us our debts, as we forgive our debtors." He was sinless. This was a prayer for His disciples and for us. And because this book is about discipleship, it is fitting that we have a clearer understanding of this prayer.

Within this prayer, we are given the principles we need to understand how to communicate with God. The disciples had watched Jesus pray. They had seen Him spend time with His Father. They had seen His intimacy and His closeness with the

Father. In contrast, they had also seen the ritualized, cold, academic prayers of the religious hypocrites.

So Jesus began His lesson on prayer by saying, "In this manner, therefore, pray . . ." (Matt. 6:9). Let me emphasize that Jesus was not giving the disciples merely a canned, formalized prayer. In fact, this prayer was never repeated in the New Testament. That is not to say that it is wrong to pray this prayer verbatim or to use it as an act of worship to God. But it should not be adhered to merely as a ritual. There is nothing magical in simply uttering it. However, we can learn from its form and structure how to pray more effectively. It is a model and pattern for all prayers.

This prayer is divided into two sections. The first three petitions focus on the glory of God, while the last three deal with our need as humans.

It should be pointed out that the prayer begins with "Our Father in heaven" and not with "Give us this day our daily bread." Too often, we begin our prayers with our needs.

"Our Father in heaven"

When we pray, we should first recognize whom we are speaking to: "Our Father in heaven" (v. 9). It is good to pause before you speak in prayer, realizing that you are addressing the Creator of the universe. Too often we rush into the presence of God and absentmindedly rattle off our petitions. We ought to first be quiet and wait before the Lord before saying anything. Then, after a time of contemplation of whom we are addressing, we then will more reverently pray, "Our Father. . . ."

Those words should remind us that it is our Father, the one who has our best interests at heart, to whom we are speaking. As 1 John 3:1 reminds us, "Behold what manner of love the Father has bestowed on us, that we should be called children of God!" From this we can be assured that whatever happens as a result, our prayer is in accordance with what our Father wants for us.

We may not always agree with what He decides, but we can be assured that His will for us is good. We know He loves us with an everlasting love.

When you have been around a little while, you begin to have the advantage of twenty-twenty hindsight. You can look back on your life and see how God's wisdom has prevailed. I can think of things that I prayed for years ago, things that I was certain were the will of God for me, and He said no. Some of those prayers were answered some time later. And some of them were never answered in the way that I prayed them. But now I can look back and say, "Lord, thank you for the way that You worked in my life."

You need to trust that your Father in heaven is doing the same for you right now. Psalm 84:11 says, "No good thing will He withhold from those who walk uprightly." Just because God is saying no doesn't mean that He is turning His back on you. It means that He is looking out for your welfare.

When we pray to our Father in heaven, it should remind us that He is the Creator. That should fill our hearts with humility and awe. Just uttering those words helps to prepare our hearts and to see our smallness in light of His greatness.

"Hallowed be Your name"

Following our acknowledgment of whom we are speaking to, the loving Father and Creator, we are then reminded of His holiness: "Hallowed be Your name" (v. 9). The word "hallowed" could also be translated "sanctified," "revered," or "holy." It recognizes that we should want to be sanctified, or set apart, for Jesus Christ to live holy lives. Because He is holy, so we also should live holy lives. All of our ambitions, interests, and pursuits should reveal that we follow a holy God.

A prayer that is powerful must be prayed for God's glory. When you read through the Scriptures, you will find that the great prayers recorded in the Bible always glorify God and set Him apart, such as

Elijah's prayer on Mount Carmel (see 1 Kings 18:36).

The privilege of prayer was not given to us so that we could demand things from God. James 4:3 tells us why some of our prayers go unanswered: "When you ask, you do not receive, because you ask with wrong motives, that you may spend what you get on your pleasures" (NIV). We should ask for the things God wants to give us. If He gave us everything we asked for, it would ultimately destroy us. We must seek His glory more than our own desires.

I have found that when I seek God's glory, His will, and His kingdom, He blesses me. It is not wrong to ask for what you believe is necessary, but I make it a point to preface my prayers with something like, "Lord, I think this would be a great thing for You to do and I really think You ought to do it, but Your will be done. If I am missing something, if there's more to this than I know, then overrule my petition. I know whatever You do will be best." That is praying with His glory in mind.

"Your kingdom come. . . ."

The next phrase in our model prayer is, "Your kingdom come. Your will be done on earth as it is in heaven" (v. 10). A person cannot pray, "Your kingdom come" until he or she can first pray, "My kingdom go."

All too often, our prayers are meant to establish our kingdom. We want to be the captain of our own ship, the master of our own destiny. This will not do if we truly want His kingdom and if we truly want to be His disciples. We must turn over the reins of leadership completely to Him.

Therefore, it is essential that we learn what the will of God is, so that we can pray for it. If you pray according to the will of God, your prayers always will be answered in the affirmative. According to 1 John 5:14–15, "Now this is the confidence that we have in Him, that if we ask anything according to His will, He hears us.

And if we know that He hears us, whatever we ask, we know that we have the petitions that we have asked of Him."

Jesus put it this way in John 15:7: "If you abide in Me, and My words abide in you, you will ask what you desire, and it shall be done for you." Literally this verse means, "I command you to ask at once for yourselves whatever you desire, and it is yours."

As we spend time in the Word of God as a disciple, learning the will of God and the desires of God, our prayers will change. They no longer will be self-centered or self-indulgent. Instead, they will be oriented toward the glory and will of God. As we align ourselves with His will and start praying for it, we will begin to see the results. Most prayers are not answered because they are outside the will of God.

Once we have discovered God's will, we can then pray aggressively and confidently for it. We can pray, believing it will happen, because we know it is not something we have dreamed up. James 1:6–7 tells us that when we pray, we should "be sure that [our] faith is in God alone. Do not waver, for a person with divided loyalty is as unsettled as a wave of the sea that is blown and tossed by the wind. Such people should not expect to receive anything from the Lord" (NLT).

When Jesus went to His hometown, we are told that "He did not do many mighty works there because of their unbelief" (Matt. 13:58). In other words, unbelief will cancel our own prayers. We must pray, believing.

So where do we get such faith? "Faith comes by hearing, and hearing by the word of God" (Rom. 10:17). I can pray, believing that God will save a person's soul, because I am told in Scripture that God is "not willing that any should perish but that all should come to repentance" (2 Peter 3:9). Therefore, I can pray, believing and hoping that God will save that individual. Nevertheless, the ultimate result is God's doing and not my praying.

I can also pray with biblical authority for revival in our country, city, home, or church. I believe this is something God wants to do, because as we have seen, it is clearly proclaimed in Scripture (see 2 Chron. 7:14). And on a more personal level, I can pray authoritatively that God would make me more like Jesus and that He would reveal His will to me (see Rom. 8:29; 12:2). The Scripture clearly mandates many things that are God's will.

"Give us this day our daily bread"

After establishing whom we are speaking to and acknowledging His rightful position, we then come to the first petition: "Give us this day our daily bread" (v. 11).

Let me again emphasize the order of Jesus' model prayer. Before a word of personal petition is uttered, Jesus shows us that we must first realize who it is we are speaking to and ask for His will above our own. God is not our heavenly butler.

Also notice that Jesus does not say, "Give us this *year* our *yearly* bread" or even, "Give us this *month* our *monthly* bread." God wants us to rely on Him *daily*! Sadly, many people do not want to depend on God; they would rather depend on themselves.

It is noteworthy that in John 6, Jesus described himself as the Bread of Life. We must seek a fresh encounter each day with Him. Yesterday's "bread" is largely useless for today, much like the manna provided by God for the children of Israel during their wilderness wanderings. The manna would not keep overnight without spoiling; it was good for that day only.

The same applies to your spiritual life. God wants to give you fresh direction each day. The Scripture tells us, "Because of the Lord's great love we are not consumed, for his compassions never fail. They are new every morning; great is your faithfulness" (Lam. 3:22–23 NIV). God wants to bring newness into your relationship with Him.

"Forgive us our debts. . . ."

We find the next petition in verse 12: "And forgive us our debts, as we forgive our debtors." A true disciple will recognize the need for confession of sin, because the Bible says that unconfessed sin will hinder prayer (see Ps. 66:18). If we hold onto or cling to sin in our lives, God will not hear us. We should always remember to ask God to forgive our sins, even those we are not aware of. After all, the only sin God cannot forgive is the one we will not confess.

Some people have misunderstood the second part of this phrase, "as we forgive our debtors." They teach that the condition of being forgiven is that we must first forgive others. I do not believe this, because it is a clear contradiction to other scriptural teachings. The only basis for receiving forgiveness from God is asking for it: "If we confess our sins, He is faithful and just to forgive us our sins and to cleanse us from all unrighteousness" (1 John 1:9).

Clearly God does not make forgiving others a prerequisite, necessarily, for being forgiven. What He is saying is this: "If you have really been forgiven and you understand something of that forgiveness, then you will be forgiving of other people." If you are not forgiving of others, then I question whether you know anything of God's forgiveness in your own life.

A forgiven person will be a forgiving person. A true disciple will harbor no grudge toward another. The disciple knows it will hinder his or her prayer life and walk with God. Let's not forget what Jesus said: "By this all will know that you are My disciples, if you have love for one another" (John 13:35).

For that reason, no child of God can walk around with bitterness, anger, or hostility in his heart toward another person without feeling the conviction of his sin. We must forgive others as we have been forgiven.

"Do not lead us into temptation. . . ."

Jesus concludes this prayer with, "And do not lead us into temptation, but deliver us from the evil one. For Yours is the kingdom and the power and the glory forever. Amen" (v. 13). The "evil one" is an obvious reference to Satan. We are to recognize our total weakness apart from God and the fact that we are engaged in a spiritual battle. We need our Father's protection. Without Him, we are completely vulnerable. We must depend on Him for daily bread, depend on His will for direction, and depend on Him for power.

ACTS

This is the model, the template for prayer that Jesus has given us. First recognize the awesomeness of God. Before saying a word, worship, adore, and thank Him for all that He has done. Pray for His will in your life, and then the rule of His kingdom in your heart as well as the hearts of others. Then having put things in their proper perspective, bring your needs before Him. Confess your sins, and forgive those who have wronged you.

Another way to remember the structure of this model prayer is to use the acronym, ACTS:

Adoration

Confession

Thanksgiving

Supplication

First I adore God and praise Him. Then I confess my sin. Next I remember to give thanks. Then I offer my supplications.

With this model prayer as our guide, we must not fail to "pray without ceasing" (1 Thess. 5:17). As we do, these essential ingredients of effective prayer will help us make great strides in being disciples of Jesus.

CHAPTER SIX
Discipleship and the Church

And the Lord added to the church daily those who were being saved. (Acts 2:42)

So far, we have looked at two essentials for our growth as disciples of Jesus Christ: Bible study and prayer.

The third essential involves the significance of the church in the life of the disciple. I cannot stress enough the importance of regular fellowship and participation in the church. As we come into the church and find our place in it, we are then in a position to give to others what God has given us. Every Christian has an important role in the body of Christ, and God has given special gifts to each one.

The emphasis, however, is not merely on what a believer gets from the church, but on what he or she can contribute. The Bible tells us to "think of ways to motivate one another to acts of love and good works. And let us not neglect our meeting together, as some people do, but encourage one another, especially now that the day of his return is drawing near" (Heb. 10:24–25 NLT).

The church is not only a place where we can be taught God's Word and where we can worship Him; it is also a place where we can come to be equipped for service.

A healthy church will be filled with believers who desire not only to receive, but to give. Rather than having an attitude that says, "Bless me; do something for me," they will want to help out. They want to follow the example of Jesus, who came not to be served, but to serve (see Matt. 20:28; Mark 10:45).

That is not to say we don't need to be ministered to and spiritually nourished when we go to church, for indeed we should. The number-one priority in selecting a church should not be how close it is to your home or how nice its facilities are. The most important thing is to ask, "Is this church teaching God's Word?" I don't just mean topical studies, but Bible exposition where you are working your way through books of the Bible. There is a place for addressing topics, but everything ought to be done from a biblical perspective. People should bring their Bibles to church and read from them in the service. The pastor should preach from the Bible as well.

But as we take in, we should also recognize our privilege and responsibility to give out. If a need or opportunity arises, we should be willing to leave our nice, comfortable seat and volunteer. The right attitude of a truly thankful Christian is, "God has given to me and, as a result, I want to give to others."

The Function of Spiritual Gifts

God has given gifts to each of us who have put our faith in Jesus Christ, and He has empowered us with the Holy Spirit. Are you using and cultivating the gifts God has given you? The Bible specifically tells us that as believers, we are to use our spiritual gifts as we await the return of Christ (see 1 Cor. 1:7).

Also, failing to discover and use the gifts God has given us could cause us to quench the Holy Spirit, which the Bible specifically commands us not to do (see 1 Thess. 5:19). "Quench" carries the idea of extinguishing something. So when God's Spirit nudges us to say or do a certain thing and we refuse, we are quenching the Spirit.

Some Christians feel adverse toward the gifts of the Spirit, probably because there is so much abuse in this area. Often those who claim to be using the gifts of the Spirit are some of the strangest people around. As a result, we conclude that if these are the gifts of the Holy Spirit, then we don't want anything to do with them.

But let's not look at the gifts that way. Let's take a step back and look at them in a biblical and balanced way. I believe in the power of the Holy Spirit, but I believe it is a practical power that God wants us to have in our lives, the same power that caused the early church to turn their world upside down.

Ephesians 4, a definitive chapter on the gifts of the Spirit, explains why God has given them: "And He Himself gave some to be apostles, some prophets, some evangelists, and some pastors and teachers, *for the equipping of the saints for the work of ministry, for the edifying of the body of Christ . . .*" (vv. 11–12, emphasis added).

First, we see that God has given the gifts of the Spirit for the perfecting, or the maturing of, the saints. God has raised up pastor-teachers, evangelists, and prophets to help us grow up, so "that we should no longer be children, tossed to and fro and carried about with every wind of doctrine, by the trickery of men, in the cunning craftiness of deceitful plotting, but, speaking the truth in love, may grow up in all things into Him who is the head—Christ" (vv. 14–15). God gives us these gifts, working through people like pastor-teachers, so we will be equipped and will mature.

Second, God has given the gifts of the Spirit so we will be equipped to do all God has called us to do in the church. God has a gift, or gifts, for you to use to bless others. The gifts of the Spirit are not a hobby to play with; they are tools to build with and weapons to fight with.

Third, God has given the gifts of the Spirit to bring unity in the church, "till we all come to the unity of the faith and of the knowledge of the Son of God, to a perfect man, to the measure of the stature of the fullness of Christ" (v. 13). As we use these gifts, we discover that no one person has all the gifts. God, in His sovereign will, has chosen to give certain gifts to certain people.

As Romans 12:4–6 reminds us, "Just as each of us has one body with many members, and these members do not all have the same function, so in Christ we who are many form one body, and each member belongs to all the others. We have different gifts, according to the grace given us" (NIV).

Fourth, God has given the gifts of the Spirit for the growth of Christians spiritually and for the growth of the church numerically: "From him the whole body, joined and held together by every supporting ligament, grows and builds itself up in love, as each part does its work" (v. 16 NIV). When a church is grounded in God's Word and energized by the Holy Spirit, it will reach out, not satisfied to stay to itself. It will permeate, challenge, and confront our culture. It is power with a purpose.

Many people have become passive spectators in the church, charter members of the "Bless Me Club." This mentality causes spiritual stagnation. God did not intend for us to take in without ever giving anything out.

Secrets of the Early Church

To better understand how we should function as disciples in the church, we need to look at the New Testament church as Jesus established it. Acts 2 records the first day in the life of the church. Here we find the first-century disciples in action. We also find principles that make for an effective church and for the true disciple's place in it.

At first glance, this text reveals that the early church was dramatically different from much of the church today. What was normal to them is radical to us. Discipleship is really "radical Christian living." Normal Christian living as presented in the New Testament was a passionate, Spirit-empowered, all-consuming devotion to God and to His Word.

We must always remember that the early church was set in motion by the Holy Spirit. To be effective Christians, we must also depend on the power of the Holy Spirit. There is a dimension of power available for every believer beyond the conversion experience. When we become Christians, the Holy Spirit takes up residence inside of us. He is there to guide us into all truth. He is there to seal us with His assurance that we are children of God.

But there is another dimension of power available to us as believers. Jesus said to His disciples, "But you shall receive power when the Holy Spirit has come upon you; and you shall be witnesses to Me in Jerusalem, and in all Judea and Samaria, and to the end of the earth" (Acts 1:8). The word Jesus used for "upon" is different from words used elsewhere when speaking of the Spirit coming inside of us. This experience is an empowering one that gives us the boldness we need to live the Christian life. It is the power to live a consistent life, the power to be bold enough to share your faith.

The early church began in the power of the Holy Spirit and continued that way. If we want to flourish and be effective in our witness for Jesus Christ, then we must begin in the power of the Spirit and stay dependent upon that power until our last day.

"They continued steadfastly. . . ."

In Acts 2:42, we find the first key to the early disciples' effectiveness: "And they continued steadfastly in the apostles' doctrine and fellowship, in the breaking of bread, and in prayers." The early Christians had an intense passion to participate in the life of the church. Not only was there passion behind their actions, but there was a consistency, a steadfastness about them. Passion and consistency were the keys to helping them do God's will.

Also, the early believers did not take for granted the privilege of meeting together. The more I travel, the more thankful I have become for what God is doing here in our country in our own churches. Pastors in Eastern Europe have told me how hard it is to do what God wants them to do with the restrictions imposed by government. Pastors in Ethiopia have told me how they and members of their congregations have been tortured and imprisoned for preaching the gospel and following Jesus. We are privileged here in the United States to have the freedoms we do. We must never take them for granted, and we must remember to pray for our brothers and sisters who live in countries where religious freedom is not tolerated.

What is your attitude toward going to church? When you go to church, do you go with an earnest hunger for the spiritual milk of God's Word (see 1 Peter 2:2)? Do you crave it? That passion certainly can make a difference. The early believers' passion was directed toward the "apostles' doctrine." The early church continued in God's Word. And as disciples, we must do the same.

Also, the early believers' passion was directed toward fellowship. We have somehow lost the true meaning of the word "fellowship." Often we hear it used at church gatherings, where there promises to be "food, fun, and fellowship." But is that what the early church was experiencing? What is fellowship, exactly?

First of all, fellowship is not merely Christian social activity. Though it may involve that to some extent, true fellowship encompasses a much greater commitment. The word used for fellowship in the New Testament is a very distinct Greek word: *koinonia*. It also can be translated "communion," "partnership," "contribution," and "distribution." Each of these words provides a different facet of *koinonia*.

In part, fellowship is a common link with another individual that includes friendship, spiritual intimacy, unity, and a partnership in doing the work of Christ here on Earth.

The word "communion" speaks of friendship and intimacy. God wants us to have friendship and intimacy not only with Him, but with one another. It is a bond that can bring Christians together like no other bond, even closer than the bond of a family. Two believers share a unique exchange as God's Spirit works in their lives.

Then there is the word "partnership," which implies cooperation. Fellowship is not only mystical communion; it is also practical. It involves helping and working with another person, as well as praying for and worshiping with that individual.

Next, there are the elements of contribution and distribution. These also imply practical help for fellow believers through the sharing of food, clothing, and other needs. The Bible tells us that if we see brothers and sisters destitute and in need and fail to help them, then we are without faith (see James 2:15–17). When confronted with such a situation, we need to obey God and help our fellow Christians. That is fellowship. We see this element of fellowship clearly at work in the early church as we read that they shared "all things in common" (see v. 44).

God delights in His people gathering together for *koinonia*. In fact, God promised to manifest himself uniquely at these times. The psalmist wrote that God inhabits the praises of Israel (see Ps. 22:3 KJV). When we, with other believers, set our eyes and hearts above our circumstances and focus on our Father, it brings everything into perspective. God's presence is uniquely sensed at those times.

God will even manifest himself in a special way in our conversations with other Christians. Malachi 3:16 tells us, "Then those who feared the Lord talked with each other, and the Lord listened and heard. A scroll of remembrance was written in his presence concerning those who feared the Lord and honored his name" (NIV). In its original Hebrew, the phrase "the Lord listened and heard" means "to prick the ear; to bend down so as not to miss a word."

In essence, God is saying, "When My people come together and speak of Me, it pricks My ear. It causes Me to come down and listen carefully so as to not miss a word." That is both exciting and frightening. You've heard it said that Jesus is the unseen listener of every conversation. Think about that. When Jesus hears us mention His name to fellow Christians, it's as though He says, "They're talking about Me. I want to hear." And if that were not enough, there is also a scroll of remembrance, written in His presence, containing the names of all those who fear the Lord and honor His name in true biblical fellowship.

Along with fellowship, the early Christians also "continued in prayers" (v. 42). The word "prayer" also could be translated "steadfast earnestness." As I pointed out in the last chapter, prayer is a key element in being a disciple of Jesus. But it is also a primary element of an effective church. The early church was characterized by steadfast, earnest prayer.

Gladness and Simplicity of Heart

The first-century disciples had "gladness and simplicity of heart" (v. 46). Are you glad when it is time to go to church? David wrote, "I was glad when they said to me, 'Let us go into the house of the Lord' " (Ps. 122:1). These days, some people could say, "I was mad when they said to me, 'Let us go into the house of the Lord' "!

I find it interesting how arguments start over going to church, especially when there is somewhere else to go. We make up a host of excuses as to why we can't go on that particular day: "It looks like it might rain today," or "It's too crowded." Yet we wouldn't think twice about going to the mall on a rainy day, even if it meant parking a mile from the entrance. It is all a matter of priorities.

I've heard the word "excuse" defined as "the skin of a reason stuffed with a lie." The early believers didn't appear to have excuses. Instead, they had "simplicity of heart." Their lives had one purpose and were pointed in one direction.

When addressing His disciples in the Sermon on the Mount, Jesus said, "The lamp of the body is the eye. If therefore your eye is good, your whole body will be full of light. But if your eye is bad, your whole body will be full of darkness. If therefore the light that is in you is darkness, how great is that darkness!" (Matt. 6:22–23). If we are set apart for God and for His singular purpose, we will be seeking Him first, and our lives will be full of light. On the other hand, if we have an eye that is dark, it means we have double vision. Though we may be looking to God, we are also looking to the world. And when we try to pursue what both God and the world have to offer, our lives will be full of darkness and confusion.

The early church focused on what was important, and they let nothing get in the way. If we allow ourselves to be consistently influenced by the things of this world, it will dull our appetite for God's Word and will pull us away from Him. It also will lessen our interest in prayer and our desire to be with God's people.

But when we are living as disciples, we will look forward to going to church on a consistent and frequent basis. Meeting with other believers will be like a spiritual oasis where we can be refreshed. It will be an occasion to encourage one another as we go out to live in this world as witnesses for Jesus Christ.

Finally, we read that "the Lord added to the church daily those who were being saved" (v. 47). A healthy church is a growing church. Likewise, a healthy believer is one who will be a shining light in this world of darkness. Even as the Lord adds to the church daily, a disciple of Jesus will be an instrument of God, drawing people to Christ by doing his or her part within the church.

Our Future Reward

One day, you will stand before God, and He will reward you for your faithfulness to Him. He will not overlook even the smallest and insignificant gesture on behalf of the kingdom of God. Jesus said that in our service to God, even if it is not seen by people, it is seen by Him: "Your Father who sees in secret will Himself reward you openly" (Matt. 6:4). Speaking of this day in the future, the Bible says, "For we must all appear before the judgment seat of Christ, that each one may receive what is due him for the things done while in the body, whether good or bad" (2 Cor. 5:10 NIV).

This is not to be confused with the Great White Throne judgment (see Rev. 20), where anyone who is not found written in the Book of Life is cast into the Lake of Fire. This Great White Throne judgment is only for the unbeliever.

We find more about the judgment seat of Christ (the Bema Seat judgment), exclusively for believers, in 1 Corinthians 3:

> For no one can lay any foundation other than the one we already have—Jesus Christ. Anyone who builds on that foundation may use a variety of materials—gold, silver, jewels, wood, hay, or straw. But on the judgment day, fire will reveal what kind of work each builder has done. The fire will show if a person's work has any value. If the work survives, that builder will receive a reward. (vv. 11–14)

According to this and other passages, our presence in the kingdom is guaranteed by the promises of God, but our position in the kingdom will be won or lost by the quality of service we render here and now. Salvation is a gift to us because we have put our faith in Jesus. Honor is a reward for service to Jesus. It is about receiving rewards for what you have done for God. The wood, hay, or straw represents squandered resources, time—and indeed, an entire life.

There is nothing wrong with having a career. But if that career was more important in your life than God, then you will have a problem. If possessions were more important than God, or a hobby, or even a ministry, then at the judgment seat of Christ, the fire will go through those things and nothing will be left to show for your life.

One day, God will want to know what you did with the gifts and talents He has given you. Every one of us has been given certain skills and talents. You have something to bring in the service of God.

Yet many times we don't use our gifts for His glory. Instead, we chase after what we want in life. The Bible teaches that we are put on this earth to bring glory to God. That is why we are here. God says, "Everyone who is called by My name, whom I have created for My glory; I have formed him, yes, I have made him" (Isa. 43:7).

Let's mark it well in our minds and hearts: We are to glorify Him in all that we do with our lives.

CHAPTER SEVEN
Discipling Others

It is not that we think we are qualified to do anything on our own. Our qualification comes from God. He has enabled us to be ministers of his new covenant.
(2 Corinthians 3:5–6 NLT)

This is the most important chapter in this book. This is what I have been building toward, for we now come to the practical result of being a disciple of Jesus Christ: passing on what we have learned and discipling others.

Prior to His ascension, Jesus gave His disciples these marching orders:

> "All authority has been given to Me in heaven and on earth. Go therefore and make disciples of all the nations, baptizing them in the name of the Father and of the Son and of the Holy Spirit, teaching them to observe all things that I have commanded you; and lo, I am with you always, even to the end of the age." (Matt. 28:18–20)

To feel the impact these orders are to have on our lives as His disciples, we must make two important observations.

First, the three verses you just read are often referred to as the Great Commission. Notice that it is a *commission* as opposed to a *suggestion*. Jesus never merely suggested that we should carry the gospel to the world. It was—and is—a command.

Second, these words were not directed only to the original

twelve disciples, nor are they meant exclusively for pastors, evangelists, and missionaries. They are for every follower and disciple of Jesus Christ. If I am His disciple, then I am commanded to go and make disciples of others. And if I am not making disciples of others, then I am not really being the disciple He wants me to be.

What, then, does it mean to make disciples? Verse 20 defines it as "teaching them to observe all things that I have commanded you." Simply put, it is not only sharing our faith with others, but it is also living out our faith so that people may observe it in action—sharing the gospel message by word and modeling it by example.

With this understanding, we now have a proper basis for examining in greater detail what it means to disciple another individual.

Empowered for the Task

Let me emphasize that God will never ask us to do anything that He will not give us the power to do. The calling of God is the enabling of God (see 2 Cor. 3:4–6). If He has commanded us to go and make disciples, then we can be confident He will be there to give us the ability to see it through.

Notice Jesus said, "All authority has been given to Me in heaven and on earth. Go therefore and make disciples." From this we see that if the power is in Jesus Christ and He is living inside us, then His power and resources are at our disposal to accomplish the task.

We all need to ask God for a strong dose of boldness from the Holy Spirit. In Acts 4:23–31, we see an interesting display of this boldness in the lives of Peter and John. As I pointed out in Chapter 2, they had been preaching the gospel, which infuriated the religious leaders. As a result, they were arrested and forbidden to ever preach again. They couldn't comply with that, however, so they prayed,

"Now, Lord, look on their threats, and grant to Your servants that with all boldness they may speak Your word, by stretching out Your hand to heal, and that signs and wonders may be done through the name of Your holy Servant Jesus." (vv. 29–30)

After they prayed, the Bible tells us the place where they were meeting was shaken, and they were filled with the Holy Spirit and spoke the word of God boldly.

Here Peter and John were in trouble for their outspokenness, so what did they do? They prayed for even greater boldness. They had laid hold of Jesus' promise to them in Acts 1:8: "But you shall receive power when the Holy Spirit has come upon you; and you shall be witnesses to Me." Most of us suddenly become "chickenhearted" when it comes to sharing the gospel. We need to ask God for the power He has made available to us.

The hardest thing about sharing your faith with unbelievers is getting started, forcing those first words out of your mouth. That is where the power of the Holy Spirit is essential. Then once the ball is rolling, you will discover that sharing your faith can become a joy as well as a great blessing. Better yet, you may play an important role in changing someone's eternal destiny.

The Salt of the Earth

Jesus concluded His own definition of discipleship in the Gospel of Luke by saying, "Salt is good; but if the salt has lost its flavor, how shall it be seasoned?" (Luke 14:34). To receive the full benefit of what Jesus was saying, we need to understand the first-century mindset. In Roman culture, salt was very important. Next to the sun, salt was the most important thing there was. Often Roman soldiers were actually paid in salt, which is where the expression, "He's not worth his salt," originates. With this in mind, Jesus is saying, "You are to be salt in this earth. You are valuable. You can make a difference."

A distinct quality of salt is that it affects everything it comes into contact with. For instance, just a little pinch of salt in a glass of water can be tasted. In the same way, even one faithful Christian in an ungodly situation or place can make a difference.

Salt also stimulates thirst. When you buy popcorn at the movie theater, you quickly discover that it has been heavily salted, probably with the intent of stimulating your thirst so you will buy a drink to go with it.

In the same way, if we live godly lives, it can stimulate spiritual thirst in the lives of others. If unbelievers see something different in you, if they see that you are not like everyone else and that you live a life directed by certain spiritual principles, they can find it very appealing. Many unbelievers are also influenced when they see a Christian face severe circumstances and still maintain a sense of calmness and peace. Our lives are the only Bible many people ever will read. Christians are to be living epistles, written by God and read by men (see 2 Cor. 3:2).

One of the greatest compliments paid to a Christian is when an unbeliever says, "What is different about you? There's a quality that I admire, and I want to know more. Tell me about what you believe." That is being salt.

On the other hand, smacking unbelievers across the head with a Bible is not being a witness for Jesus. A more effective witness would be to let those unbelievers around you watch and see the difference God has made in your life. Even something as subtle as taking your Bible to work and reading it quietly during lunch or on your break could have a great impact.

Jesus has called us to be fishers of men, and one thing that is helpful in fulfilling that role is to first throw out the bait. If I want to start a conversation with the person next to me on a plane, I will often pull out my Bible and set it on the tray. Some people look at me as though I have a highly contagious disease, and they want to quickly move. But there are others who will ask what I am reading. This often opens the door to share God's truth.

When you want to share your faith with someone, it is generally a good idea to first talk about how God is working in your own life. Give people an opportunity, and if they respond, reel them in a bit by telling them a little more about Jesus. If their interest continues to grow, you can then explain what it means to know Christ, what Christ did, and what our response should be to Him.

Sometimes the conversation will come to a point where someone doesn't want to hear any more. If that is the case, don't push it. As 2 Timothy 2:24–25 says,

> And the Lord's servant must not quarrel; instead, he must be kind to everyone, able to teach, not resentful. Those who oppose him he must gently instruct, in the hope that God will grant them repentance leading them to a knowledge of the truth. (NIV)

You can come to a point where a person has heard enough. That is the time to simply pull back and say, "If you want to know more, just read the Bible, and I'll pray for you." I often recommend reading the Gospel of John, because it was written so that we may believe that Jesus was the Son of God (see John 20:31). In the future, maybe that person who was once resistant will start the conversation again.

The Bible says we are to be "as shrewd as snakes and as innocent as doves" (Matthew 10:16 NIV). We are to have wisdom without being overly aggressive. Some Christians try to stuff the gospel down people's throats, but that approach never works. Others argue and use pressure tactics to coerce a person into the kingdom of God. I suppose they feel the end justifies the means. But keep this in mind: If people can be argued into believing, they also can be argued out. If they can be pressured in, they also can be pressured out. Our responsibility as Christians is simply to proclaim the truth of the gospel and leave the conversion process to God.

The Light of the World

Jesus used two analogies to show the impact Christians should have in this world: salt and light. We have already seen what salt does. In contrast to being salt, which is primarily living what you believe, light signifies proclaiming what you believe.

Jesus said, "Let your light shine before men, that they may see your good deeds and praise your Father in heaven" (Matt. 5:16). Too many believers try to be light without first being salt. They talk the Christian talk, but they don't walk the Christian walk. Quite honestly, it would be better if they didn't say a thing if they are unable to back it up with their lifestyle.

In contrast, there are those who are salt without being light. They live godly lives, but they don't tell people why. We must find the balance. Romans 10:14 says, "How then shall they call on Him in whom they have not believed? And how shall they believe in Him of whom they have not heard? And how shall they hear without a preacher?" God wants us to be instruments through which He can speak.

There is a right way and a wrong way to share the gospel message. Therefore, it is important to rely on Jesus and let Him guide us. I believe that God wants us to be sharpshooters, not machine gunners. I have seen machine-gun evangelists who gauge their success by how many people they can talk to in one hour. If you are doing that instead of really taking time with someone, then it may not have any real or lasting effect. It may even drive people away.

I have found that the most effective sharing takes time. It is far better to sit down for an hour and talk genuinely with one person than to rattle off trite clichés to scores of people. Some of the most profound things Jesus ever said were in one-on-one conversations. His talks with the Samaritan woman (see John 4:5–42) and with Nicodemus (see John 3:1–21) have become our scripts for evangelism. Jesus took time for these individuals, so how much more should we take time for those we are speaking with?

We need to learn to let God's Holy Spirit lead as we share our faith. When a person comes to Christ, it will be a result of God's work, not our own. Jesus said, "No one can come to Me unless it has been granted to him by My Father" (John 6:65). No brilliant argument ever will win over another person. It must be the work of the Holy Spirit, and it must be in God's timing. Scripture tells us, "Preach the word! Be ready in season and out of season. Convince, rebuke, exhort, with all longsuffering and teaching" (2 Tim. 4:2). Or, as another translation puts it, "Be prepared, whether the time is favorable or not" (NLT). We need to always be ready, because we never know when we will be called into action.

A State of Readiness

Think of Philip, whom God simply told to go to the desert (see Acts 8:26–40). He didn't tell him there would be a wealthy and powerful man from Ethiopia who would be searching for God and waiting for him when he arrived. He just told him to go to the desert. Philip obeyed, and upon his arrival, he found the man. His timing was just right. If Philip had lagged behind or run ahead, he would have missed out on the opportunity to lead this man to Christ.

Often we miss out on opportunities that God brings our way simply because we are not paying attention. Undoubtedly, God can get the job done without us. He will find someone else, but we will miss out on the privilege of being used by Him.

We can also learn a great deal from Philip's methods. He asked this Ethiopian an interesting question when he heard him reading from the writings of the prophet Isaiah: "Do you understand what you are reading?" (v. 30). The Ethiopian responded by saying, "How can I, unless someone guides me?" (v. 31).

Do We Care Enough to Share?

Do you share your faith with others on a regular basis? If not, why not? If most Christians today were brutally honest, many of us would have to admit that we really don't care about the plight of the unbeliever. The apostle Paul said, "Yet preaching the Good News is not something I can boast about. I am compelled by God to do it. How terrible for me if I didn't preach the Good News!" (1 Cor. 9:16 NLT).

Evangelism must start with a genuine concern for the lost. The people we talk to can tell when we are sincere. Paul had such a concern. He was so stirred for his own people to come to Christ that he said, "My heart is filled with bitter sorrow and unending grief for my people, my Jewish brothers and sisters. I would be willing to be forever cursed—cut off from Christ!—if that would save them" (Rom. 9:2–3 NLT). Paul was saying he was willing to be cut off from Christ himself if he could be confident that his fellow Jews would come to know Him.

Moses had the same heart for Israel. We read in Exodus 32 that Moses went to Mount Sinai to receive the commandments of God. But when days passed and Moses had not returned to the camp, the people grew desperate and looked for a replacement for God in their lives. Under the misdirected leadership of Aaron, a golden calf was made and the people began to worship it.

As the sinful activity of the people was unfolding, God told Moses, "Go, get down! For your people whom you brought out of the land of Egypt have corrupted themselves" (v. 7).

God went on to speak about the guilt of the people, and Moses interrupted Him with a cry of intercession: "Lord, why does Your wrath burn hot against Your people whom You have brought out of the land of Egypt with great power and with a mighty hand?" (v. 11).

"They are *your* people," God said to Moses.

"No, they are *Your* people," Moses replied to God.

It is obvious that neither Moses nor God wanted these people in the condition they were in at that particular moment: naked and dancing around a golden calf. When Moses came down to the camp and saw this horrible spectacle, he, in righteous indignation, smashed the tablets God had given him.

The next day, Moses started back up the mountain with great determination in his heart. When he reached the top, he began to speak to God. The statement the burdened prophet made to Him is very significant. It is a sigh, a groan, a cry. It is a sentence that has no ending. Even in the King James Version, the translators left the end of the sentence trailing, using a dash for punctuation. You might say it was a sentence that was broken in the middle by the sobs of a man who was asking to be sent to hell . . . if only the people might be spared the righteous indignation of a holy God: "Then Moses returned to the Lord and said, 'Oh, these people have committed a great sin, and have made for themselves a god of gold! Yet now, if You will forgive their sin—'" (vv. 31–32). At this point, the sentence stops and the translators end it with a dash. It must have been a long pause, as Moses was no doubt considering the full implications of what he was asking. He went on to say, "But if not, I pray, blot me out of Your book which You have written" (v. 32).

As you can see, Moses had a tremendous burden for the people he was praying for, and he was willing to stand in the gap. God, speaking of His desire to find people with such a burden, said, "So I sought for a man among them who would make a wall, and stand in the gap before Me on behalf of the land, that I should not destroy it; but I found no one" (Ezek. 22:30).

The great Christian writer Alexander McClaren penned these words: "You tell me the depth of a Christian's compassion, and I will tell you the measure of his usefulness."

Flexibility Is Key

In 1 Corinthians 9, Paul gives us a key to effectively sharing our faith:

"When I am with those who are weak, I share their weakness, for I want to bring the weak to Christ. Yes, I try to find common ground with everyone, doing everything I can to save some. I do everything to spread the Good News and share in its blessings." (vv. 22–23 NLT)

We could sum up this aspect of evangelism in one word: flexibility. You need to adapt yourself to other people. Jesus is our supreme example in this. Have you ever noticed that He never spoke to any two people in exactly the same way? He saw people as individuals. Some Christians share the great truths of the gospel as if it were coming off a teleprompter. They simply regurgitate all the information they have memorized. Memorizing Scripture, knowing what you believe, and being able to present it effectively is right and good, but we also need to be sensitive to the people we are speaking to.

When Jesus talked to Pontius Pilate, the Roman leader asked him questions. Jesus responded to Pilate's interest. He spoke to Pilate about truth. But when Jesus was brought before Herod, He remained silent. Jesus saw genuine curiosity in Pilate and responded accordingly. In contrast, Jesus knew Herod had no real interest in spiritual things. Herod wanted to be dazzled, not changed. We, too, need to be discerning and refrain from offering the truths of God to someone who is not actually interested.

Jesus made these distinctions when He talked to other people as well. When Nicodemus came to Him and said, "No one can do these signs that You do unless God is with him" (John 3:2), Jesus got straight to the point and in essence said, "Look, Nicodemus, let's get down to brass tacks: You must be born again." There are times when God will have us do the same. I have walked up to complete strangers and said, "Has anyone ever told you about Jesus Christ? I would like to share Him with you."

There have been other times, however, when I have felt it was best not to take that approach. We see this with Jesus and the Samaritan woman. He sat down at a well in Samaria as she came to draw water at noon. She chose to make her trip to the well at that time of day because she was an outcast of society. She had been divorced a number of times and was presently living with a man she wasn't married to. And not only that, she was a Samaritan.

In those days, many of the Jews looked down on Samaritans because of racial prejudice. Nevertheless, Jesus walked over to the well and sat down. As the woman was drawing water, Jesus asked her for a drink.

She turned and looked at Him in amazement, saying, "How is it that You, being a Jew, ask a drink from me, a Samaritan woman?" (John 4:9).

Then Jesus threw out a little bait by saying, "If you knew the gift of God, and who it is who says to you, 'Give Me a drink,' you would have asked Him, and He would have given you living water" (v. 10).

Having caught her interest, she then responded, "Where then do You get that living water?" (v. 11).

There are times I have found this to work very well. In the course of a conversation with an unbeliever, I might say, "I'm glad that God is in control of my life." That will usually get a little reaction. One eyebrow goes up, they look at their watch, and perhaps go on their way as quickly as possible. Or, they might say, "What do you mean, 'God is in control of your life'?" These types of statements can act as bait to get attention. If someone is interested, you can then go a little further.

Use Tact

I have often heard unbelievers blast Christians for their lack of tact. Sometimes it ends up in name-calling, and the Christian goes away feeling that he or she has been persecuted. But it is not persecution if Christians have simply been irresponsible and insensitive in their methods of sharing Christ.

A good example of the right way to witness comes from the story of Philip and the Ethiopian eunuch, which we looked at earlier in this chapter. The Ethiopian had come to Jerusalem searching for God, but sadly he did not find Him in the empty religion of the day. He did, however, pick up one very valuable item during his visit. He obtained a scroll containing the Book of Isaiah. During his ride home, he was reading aloud from Isaiah 53, one of the great messianic chapters that speaks of Jesus.

At this time, God directed Philip to this powerful, wealthy, yet empty and searching man. The way Philip approached him is a good illustration of using tact.

Tact is intuitively knowing how to say the right thing at the right time. Philip simply said to this man, "Do you understand what you are reading?" He could have said, "Did you know that you are going to be judged by God and thrown into hell? What do you think about that?" But because Philip was sensitive to this man's need, he had an open door to share the gospel.

Have Some Heart

Another aspect of effective witnessing involves the heart. When Jesus came into contact with people, He genuinely loved them. He took an interest in them. Heartfelt concern will speak volumes to someone before you even utter a word. There are so very few people who really care anymore. Everyone seems to have ulterior motives—they want something from you. As a result, we have a world that is suspicious of anyone who talks with them.

Once I was given two tickets to Disneyland. Because I was meeting some friends inside the park, I didn't need two tickets—I only needed one. As I walked in, I began to feel guilty that I was wasting a free ticket. After all, maybe there was someone who really wanted to go into the park but couldn't afford it. So I left and found some kids in the parking lot and offered the ticket to them. Their response was typical of anyone who has grown cynical about "free" offers: "What do you mean? Why are you giving me that ticket?" They didn't want it. It took nearly 30 minutes before I finally found someone who was willing to take the ticket.

The world today is flooded with religious cults. Satan is no fool. He has put so many imitations out there that unbelievers are suspicious of anyone who talks about God. These counterfeit Christians are out in full force in airports, malls, and on the streets, sharing what they perceive to be the truth. We may not like what they are saying or the way they are misrepresenting God, yet we must ask ourselves, *When was the last time I properly represented God?*

Jesus truly loved people, and we must do the same. That is our edge. The cults don't have Jesus' real love for people. We, however, have His love operating in our lives, because "the love of God has been poured out in our hearts by the Holy Spirit who was given to us" (Rom. 5:5).

One of Your Most Powerful Tools

You already possess one of the most effective tools for communicating your faith: your testimony (how you came to know Christ personally). If you go through the Book of Acts and read some of the great evangelistic messages of the apostle Paul, you will find that he often used his personal testimony. Certainly his was a dramatic one, but God can also use your personal testimony because it is unique.

Through your personal testimony, you can relay thoughts and feelings that others can easily relate to. Having established that common ground, you can then share how God has worked in your life. In this way, you come back to the central message: Jesus Christ and Him crucified.

Once you have the opportunity to share the gospel, it is important to point people to Scripture. But which verses should you share? At the back of this book, I have included a Plan of Salvation that includes key verses you might want to memorize.

True Discipleship

The full concept of discipleship is to share our faith, lead people to Christ, and then help them mature. But somewhere along the line, we have separated evangelism from discipleship. There is no such distinction in Scripture, however. The idea is not just to pray with someone and send them on their way. It is to help that new believer grow spiritually and become a dedicated, committed, fruitful, and mature disciple of Jesus Christ. Then we trust that believer will repeat the process with someone else. And so the cycle continues.

After Saul's conversion, there was great doubt among the believers as to whether he had really come to genuine faith in Christ. Saul was one of the prime persecutors of the early church. He presided over the first execution of a Christian in the New Testament, a young man named Stephen. Upon hearing that the notorious Saul had become a believer, the disciples were afraid it was just a ploy to find out where they met so he could turn them over to the authorities. But God spoke to a man named Ananias and told him to go and visit Saul. Ananias obeyed, found Saul (who later changed his name to Paul), and took the time to pray for him and encourage him (see Acts 9:10–19).

Then God brought a man named Barnabas into Paul's life. Barnabas introduced Paul to the apostles and personally reassured them that his conversion was sincere.

This is a good illustration of true discipleship. Discipling someone is not just teaching; it's also being a friend. Sadly, I find that many people who first accept Christ often fall through the cracks because no one helps them become established in the faith. It can be difficult for these people to get acclimated to church.

New believers may come to church for the first time and be encouraged by the wonderful fellowship, but when the Bible study starts and they hear something like, "Turn to Matthew 5," they immediately feel lost because they don't have the faintest idea where to look.

That is exactly how I felt when I began attending church. I remember how I didn't understand the language of the Christians. They had their own unique vocabulary—you might call it *Christianese*. I thank God that a believer saw me and took me under his wing. He invited me to church and introduced me to his Christian friends. After the services, he explained what different things meant and answered my questions.

In Acts 18, we find the story of Aquila and Priscilla, who exemplify how we should help new converts. They saw a young man named Apollos who was filled with enthusiasm for the things of God. However, he needed more insight into what he was teaching. Aquila and Priscilla took him into their home and "explained to him the way of God more accurately" (v. 26). As a result, Apollos became even more effective in what God had called him to do.

When we lead someone to Christ or meet a new Christian, we must take the initiative to see that they are stabilized in their newfound faith. Take them to church with you, introduce them to your friends, and, most importantly, be a friend.

New believers not only need to hear the truth; they need to see it lived. They can't necessarily get that from a pulpit. They need to see it in the lifestyle of a person in day-to-day living. Obviously, they will have many questions: How does a Christian act at work? How does a Christian behave when he drives? How does a Christian treat his wife and children? How does a Christian spend his free time? What movies does a Christian see? These are all a part of the discipleship process.

A mature believer can be a model for applying the truths of God. As Colossians 1:28 says, "Him we preach, warning every man and teaching every man in all wisdom, that we may present every man perfect in Christ Jesus."

The Bible offers numerous examples of this discipling process. With young Timothy, Paul repeated the discipling process he had gone through. Elijah discipled Elisha. Moses discipled Joshua. And most notably, Jesus discipled His apostles. In speaking of this process, Paul said in 1 Thessalonians 2:11, "For you know that we dealt with each of you as a father deals with his own children, encouraging, comforting and urging you to live lives worthy of God" (NIV).

One thing that keeps Christians from being active disciples is the fear of not having sufficient Bible knowledge. It is not necessary that you be a Bible scholar to lead others to Christ and disciple them. Remember, you probably know a lot more than a brand-new believer does. You can begin by sharing the building blocks of the Christian life that this book talks about: how to study the Bible, how to pray, the importance of involvement in the church, and how to live a godly life. Your life can impact a new believer's life in a wonderful way.

Benefits of Disciplemaking

The discipling of others is extremely important in the life of a disciple, because the failure to do so will have damaging results on your own walk with Christ. Attending more Bible studies, more prayer meetings, reading more Christian books, and listening to more teaching without an outlet for the truth will cause us to spiritually decay. We need to take what God has given us and use it constructively in the lives of others.

When you take a new believer under your wing, you are not only encouraging a new child of God, but you are saving yourself from spiritual stagnation. New believers need our wisdom, knowledge, and experience, and we need the zeal, spark, and childlike simplicity of faith that a young Christian possesses.

Have you ever led anyone to Jesus Christ? Have you discipled anyone? Have you taken any new believer under your wing and helped him or her along? If you do, it will reignite your spiritual life as that person discovers the truths of God for the first time (and as you rediscover them too).

Children are the best illustration of this process. When you are with a child, you begin to see things through a child's eyes again. As the child discovers things for the first time, you rediscover the newness of those things. It is wonderful when a child first discovers the ocean, walks on sand, picks up snow, or tastes ice cream. These are things we adults take for granted, but when we see a child discover them, we share in his or her excitement.

In the same way, when we see a new believer discover things from God's Word and the excitement it brings, it reignites us. Often they will ask difficult questions that will make us search the Scriptures for answers. And there are always things we have learned but forgotten. A new believer's questions can help us to rediscover (or discover for the first time) many important spiritual truths.

The fact is, many mature Christians come to a point where they simply dry up. When this happens, many begin wondering what is wrong with them. Some seek a solution in finding a new church or some new teaching that supposedly will revolutionize their lives. In most cases, the real problem is simply spiritual sluggishness. The person in this position should be passing along what he or she has learned to a younger believer. We have a choice: evangelize or fossilize.

Jesus said that "whoever has [or is passing it on], will be given more, and he will have abundance. Whoever does not have [is not passing it on], even what he has will be taken away from him" (Matt. 13:12 NIV). I have found that the more I give, the more God seems to give back to me. As Proverbs 11:25 says, "The generous soul will be made rich, and he who waters will also be watered himself."

At one point the children of Israel were facing the problem of spiritual stagnation. God told them through the prophet Isaiah to get their eyes off their own problems and start giving away what they had been given: "No, this is the kind of fasting I want: Free those who are wrongly imprisoned; lighten the burden of those who work for you. Let the oppressed go free, and remove the chains that bind people" (Isa. 58:6 NLT).

His promise to them for being obedient is found a few verses later: "Then your salvation will come like the dawn, and your wounds will quickly heal. Your godliness will lead you forward, and the glory of the Lord will protect you from behind" (v. 8 NLT).

You can be a partaker of that same promise if you will open up your life to disciple someone else. It can start today, right where you are, with the people God has brought into your life. Remember, it takes one to make one.

For the sake of those who don't yet know Christ, don't forsake God's command to "go and make disciples." For the sake of a young believer, don't let apathy rob you of being a blessing to him or her. And for the sake of maintaining an exciting, fruitful walk with God, don't ignore these commands of Jesus. The promises and blessings are for those who will apply these principles.

Indeed, the harvest is plentiful, but the laborers are few. We need more laborers, more disciples. May God help you and me to be just that.

CHAPTER EIGHT

Discipleship: It's Your Choice

And this is eternal life, that they may know You, the only true God, and Jesus Christ whom You have sent. (John 17:3)

It has been said that if you aim at nothing, you are bound to hit it. What course are you following in life? It is not a mystical thing; you decide what it will be. You have a choice in the matter.

As God said to the people of Israel:

> This day I call heaven and earth as witnesses against you that I have set before you life and death, blessings and curses. Now choose life, so that you and your children may live and that you may love the Lord your God, listen to his voice, and hold fast to him. For the Lord is your life. (Deut. 30:19–20)

The stand you make today will determine the stand you make tomorrow. You decide what the evening of your life will be by the morning of it. And the good news is that even if you have made mistakes in the past, you can still recommit yourself, because you serve the God of second chances.

You were placed on Earth to know God. Everything else is secondary. Your career, your possessions, even your ministries, are all a distant second to knowing God. Jesus prayed for His disciples, "This is eternal life, that they may know you, the only true God and Jesus Christ whom you have sent" (John 17:13).

God said to Jeremiah: "Let not the wise man glory in his wisdom, let not the mighty man glory in his might, nor let the rich man glory in his riches; but let him who glories glory in this, that he understands and knows Me" (Jer. 9:23–24).

This was the objective of the apostle Paul, who said, "I want to know Christ and the power of his resurrection and the fellowship of sharing in his sufferings, becoming like him in his death" (Phil. 3:10 NIV). Another translation states it, "That I may progressively become more deeply and intimately acquainted with Him . . ." (AMP).

Total Commitment

From his deathbed, David had these final words for his son Solomon, and they still speak powerfully to us today:

> "And Solomon, my son, learn to know the God of your ancestors intimately. Worship and serve him with your whole heart and a willing mind. For the Lord sees every heart and knows every plan and thought. If you seek him, you will find him. But if you forsake him, he will reject you forever." (1 Chron. 28:9 NLT)

David happened to know what he was talking about. When he was just a boy, He had been plucked from obscurity to become the king of Israel. One has only to read the Psalms, most of which David penned, to discover that he loved God deeply. This was a young man who enjoyed an extraordinary intimacy with God. That is why the Bible describes him as the "sweet psalmist of Israel" (2 Sam. 23:1) and "a man after [God's] own heart" (1 Sam. 13:14). We read of him tending his sheep out in the fields and singing beautiful songs of praise to God as he played his stringed instrument.

He was so adept at this that when King Saul was being tormented by demonic forces, David would play his instrument for him in praise to God, and it would temporarily drive those forces away. David enjoyed closeness with God and had no idea as he tended his sheep that God would one day call him to become the next king of Israel.

Of course he had many challenges to face before he ascended the throne. But when his day finally came, he ruled well and with wisdom. He was a courageous warrior and was well-loved by the people. God had blessed him.

But then David started to slip. The intimacy and closeness we read about in the early phases of his life is gone, and instead we see idleness. In fact, on the fateful night when he fell into sin with Bathsheba, we read, "At the time when kings go out to battle . . . David remained at Jerusalem" (2 Sam. 11:1). Instead of being out in the fields leading his troops into battle, he was kicking back and taking a little R and R. He was looking for trouble and found it in the beautiful Bathsheba. The Bible doesn't fault Bathsheba, but clearly places the blame at the feet of this young king. He was responsible for his actions.

David brought Bathsheba into his chambers, had sexual relations with her, and she became pregnant. But instead of acknowledging his sin, he had her husband Uriah brought home to make it appear as though the child were his. But Uriah didn't sleep with his wife, so David basically had Uriah put to death, covered it up (or so he thought), and then married Bathsheba. David thought he had pulled it off. A year passed in which he was out of fellowship with God. Then one day, the prophet Nathan confronted David and he came clean, admitting that he had sinned.

In spite of this tragic fall into sin, the Bible tells us that David was a man after God's own heart. Why is that? Didn't he commit some serious sins? Absolutely. But when he was confronted with his sin, he admitted it. He did not minimize his sin, nor did he blame it on others. He did not label it as something else. Instead he said to the prophet Nathan, "I have sinned against the Lord" (2 Sam. 12:13).

If you want to be a man or woman after God's own heart,

know this: you will sin. You will fall short. But when you realize you have sinned, don't blame others. Don't make excuses for it. Don't minimize it. Say, like David, "Against You, You only, have I sinned, and done this evil in Your sight" (Ps. 51:4). God will forgive you if you will confess your sin to Him (see 1 John 1:9).

Of course, that doesn't mean you won't reap the consequences of that sin in the years to come. David certainly did. Although God forgave him, he saw his own behavior repeated in the lives of his children. He was a man who had learned his lessons in the school of hard knocks.

So when he realized his life was drawing to a close, he essentially told Solomon, "Son, I am on my way out of here. You will be taking over. Here is what I have learned: You need to know God. If you understand this, everything else will fall into place. Solomon, you cannot live off my relationship with God. You must develop your own."

Note that David told Solomon to "worship and serve [God] with your whole heart and a willing mind." Or, as another translation puts it, "Serve [God] with wholehearted devotion and with a willing mind" (NIV). In other words, our commitment to God needs to be a total one.

This was a problem Abraham had when he was called by God. Like David, he had a relationship with God and was called "the friend of God." At God's command, Abraham left his pagan country and family members for a foreign land that God promised to show him. Abraham obeyed God—sort of. He did leave his country, but he took along some family members who were dragging him down spiritually. Ultimately he made that break, specifically with his nephew Lot. It was after this that God came to him again and recommissioned him.

Abraham threw away many years he could have spent drawing closer to God, because he only partially obeyed Him. Abraham had been attempting to know God with a divided heart, and God doesn't like that. He wants complete commitment to Him.

It would be like saying to your spouse, "Honey, I love you, but I am thinking of dating other people. Are you good with that?" Of course not. No one in their right mind would accept such an arrangement.

As for Solomon, he followed his father's advice in the beginning. When God appeared to him in a dream and said, "Ask! What shall I give you?" (1 Kings 3:5), Solomon replied,

> "I am a little child; I do not know how to go out or come in. . . . Therefore give to Your servant an understanding heart to judge Your people, that I may discern between good and evil. For who is able to judge this great people of Yours?" (vv. 7, 9)

God told him that because he did not ask for riches, honor, or a long life, He would give Solomon the wisdom he had asked for. What's more, God promised to bless him with the things he hadn't asked for. Solomon got off to a great start. He had such incredible wisdom that people came from around the globe to see him. No less than the Queen of Sheba told him, "Indeed, not even half the greatness of your wisdom was told me; you have far exceeded the report I heard" (2 Chron. 6:9 NIV). Solomon was on a roll. The Lord had blessed him. He was even able to build a temple for the Lord that his father David had originally wanted to build.

But as time passed, Solomon got away from knowing God. He followed in the footsteps of his father and, in some ways, was even worse. He went into a gross backslide. He had been there, done that, and bought the T-shirt. And at the end of it all, he concluded: "Fear God and keep His commandments, for this is man's all." (Eccl. 12:13). I believe Solomon came to recognize the wisdom of his father's admonition to know God.

How to Know God

So how does one know God, exactly? We have been learning the essentials of knowing God—the essentials of discipleship—throughout this book:

We know God through the careful study of His Word. It is in the Bible that we discover the character and nature of God. It is in the Bible that we learn about what is right and wrong, about what is good and evil. We don't discover these things by voting on them or by what is currently acceptable in our culture. We discover them by studying God's Word. You cannot know God without regular study of the Bible. And if you begin to neglect this, your spiritual life ultimately will start unraveling. Everything you need to know about God is found in the Bible.

We know God through prayer and worship. We need to get past the formalities and gain a true understanding of what prayer is about. The objective of prayer is not to get God to do what we want Him to do; it is to get us to do what God wants us to do. It is to get our will in alignment with His. If you can discover that, then your prayers will start being answered more often in the affirmative. Seek to spend time in prayer, because that is how you are going to know God.

We know God through worship. Worship is far more than something we do when we gather with other believers and sing songs of praise. The word "worship" has its origins in the old English word *worthship*. It means to ascribe value or worth to someone or something. In describing heaven, the apostle John wrote,

> Then I looked, and I heard the voice of many angels around the throne, the living creatures, and the elders; and the number of them was ten thousand times ten thousand, and thousands of thousands, saying with a loud voice: "Worthy is the Lamb who was slain to receive power and riches and wisdom, and strength and honor and glory and blessing!" (Rev. 5:11–12).

We worship God because He is worthy—not because we are in the mood to worship.

We know God through fellowship with other believers. The first-century believers met on a regular basis, not just once a week. I have never understood Christians who think, *I'm going to make my appearance once a week, and that will be the extent of it.* If that is your focus, then you are missing out on something. There is so much more. When we read about the church in the New Testament, we see that they met regularly and with passion. They "continued steadfastly. . . ." They were there, helping out and loving and knowing God.

It Starts with Us

The more we know God, the more we should want to make Him known to a lost world. As we look at our world today, as we look at our nation, it is easy for us to say, "America needs revival." But let's narrow it down. Revival starts with you and me. We need to revisit 2 Chronicles 7:14, where God says,

> "If My people who are called by My name will humble themselves, and pray and seek My face, and turn from their wicked ways, then I will hear from heaven, and will forgive their sin and heal their land."

Carefully pore over the words of this verse. Commit it to memory. We all want to see our land healed. But notice that God directs His words to *His* people. God doesn't point His finger at Congress or the White House. He doesn't point His finger at Hollywood. He says, "If My people. . . ." We need to ask God if there is anything in our lives that isn't right with Him. That is where we need to be looking right now.

God says, "For I know the thoughts that I think toward you, . . . thoughts of peace and not of evil, to give you a future and a hope" (Jer. 29:11). The word "future" also could be translated "an expected end," or "hope in your final outcome" (AMP). In other words, there will be an outcome, a completion in your life. God will tie up the loose ends. As a Christian, you are a work in progress: "He who has begun a good work in you will complete it until the day of Jesus Christ" (Phil. 1:6).

I am an artist. I like to draw and design and have always been interested in graphics. There have been times when I am drawing something, and someone will look over my shoulder and ask, "What's it going to be?"

"Just wait," I say.

"I think you should do this. . . ."

"Just let me do it," I tell them. "When I am finished, I will gladly show it to you."

In the same way, each of us is a work in progress. God is doing a work in your life, and when it is done, He will show you. But it is not done yet, so be patient. God sees the end from the beginning. Ecclesiastes 3:11 says, "He has made everything beautiful in its time. Also He has put eternity in their hearts, except that no one can find out the work that God does from beginning to end."

We can't see the work God is doing, but He is indeed working. One day we will be free from the effects of sin, and we no longer will experience the limitations of the human body. Our questions no longer will remain unanswered, and we will live forever in the presence of God Almighty.

In the meantime, we should make it our aim to live godly lives, which means doing what God tells us to do. This cannot be overemphasized today. We have no right to say we know God if we don't seek to live the way that He has called us to live.

Talk is cheap. I believe in verbally proclaiming the gospel, but our lifestyle is vitally important. Many times our words carry no weight, because we contradict it by the way that we live. As 1 John 2:3–4 reminds us, "And we can be sure that we know him if we obey his commandments. If someone claims, 'I know God,' but doesn't obey God's commandments, that person is a liar and is not living in the truth" (NLT).

This means that as Christians, we ought to tell the truth. It means that we should not steal. It means that we should keep our marriage vows. It means we are to be men and women of integrity, because people are watching us. It is amazing how many people will say they know God, but they don't do what He says.

Jesus said, "Let your light so shine before men, that they may see your good works and glorify your Father in heaven" (Matt. 5:16). This means that we should do good for others, including unbelievers, in the hope they will come to Christ. As I pointed out earlier, you are the only Bible some people ever will read.

When we are living godly lives, it earns us the right to proclaim the gospel boldly. People can see we are changed, and therefore, they are far more open to hearing our message.

Saved Soul, Wasted Life

All this may seem like Christianity 101, but my question is, are you doing these things? Does your life have any spiritual substance? The prophet Daniel said to the wicked king Belshazzar, who basically thumbed his nose God, "You have been weighed in the balances, and found wanting" (Dan. 5:27). In other words, "Belshazzar, you have been a spiritual lightweight. You have no substance. And now your life is required of you." His life was wasted, and it was too late. Let that not be said of us.

If your life were to be weighed in the balances today, what would God say? Would he find a life of substance, a life dedicated to following Christ? Or, would he find a life that has been wasted in empty pursuits?

As a young man, Alan Redpath was a successful CPA. He had made a commitment to Christ, but was not really living for the Lord as he should have been. One day, he was talking with a Christian friend who made a statement that would alter the course of his life: "It is possible to have a saved soul and a wasted life." Redpath could not forget those words. They haunted him all that day, into the night, and throughout the next day. He couldn't let them go. He realized that God was showing him that he had a saved soul but a wasted life. So Redpath went to his knees and prayed, "Lord, I want Your will for me. I don't want to waste my life. I dedicate it to You." God redirected his course, and instead of being a CPA, Redpath became a minister and served God for many years—which included writing a number of wonderful Christian books.

I am not suggesting that if you dedicate your life to God, He will redirect you to become a minister or a missionary, although He could. He might leave you right where you are, but show you a new way to use your gifts for His glory. Then again, He might direct you to take another path you have never even considered.

But here is what it comes down to: Your life belongs to God. You don't happen to be sharing your time and talents with Him; He is sharing them with you. You need to recognize and acknowledge that fact.

The attitude of a true disciple should be, "Lord, I don't know how much time I have left. I may have many years. Or, I may not have as many as I hope to have. Either way, my time is in Your hands. I dedicate myself to You. You have given me the sacred trust of getting the gospel message out. I am ready to do my part."

Are you willing to make this commitment today?

My prayer is that the principles I have outlined in this book will help you to better understand what it means to be a true disciple of Jesus Christ—and that you might experience radical Christian living for yourself.

Afterword

Have you ever wondered why God put you on this earth in the first place? Why were you created? What is your purpose in life?

Our primary purpose in life is to know and love God. The Book of Revelation tells us that God created all things, and by [His] will they were created and have their being" (Rev. 4:11 NIV). What a thought! God has called us, before everything else, to know Him personally and to walk with Him, with the beautiful byproduct of bringing Him pleasure. I'll let you in on a little secret: It will bring you pleasure as well.

Do you know God today? Maybe you cannot say with absolute assurance that you know Him. That is important, because if you don't know God today, He won't know you in that final day when you stand before Him. If you want to be sure you will go to heaven, you must have this relationship with God. There has to be a moment in your life where you say, "I am a sinner. I am sorry for that sin." There has to be a moment in your life when you turn from that sin and put your faith in Jesus Christ as your Savior and Lord.

If you have not done that, will you do it today? Simply say a prayer like this one, and mean it in your heart:

Dear Lord Jesus, I know I am a sinner. I believe you died for my sins. Right now, I turn from my sins and open the door of my heart and life. I confess you as my personal Lord and Savior. Thank you for saving me. Amen.

The Bible tells us, "If we confess our sins, he is faithful and just to forgive us our sins and cleanse us from all unrighteousness" (1 John 1:9). If you just prayed that prayer and meant it, then Jesus Christ has now taken residence in your heart. Your decision to follow Christ means God has forgiven you and that you will spend eternity in heaven.

To help you grow in your newfound faith, be sure to make the following a part of your life each day: reading the Bible, praying, spending time with other Christians by going to church, and telling others about your faith in Christ.

For additional resources to help you learn more about what it means to be a follower of Jesus Christ, please visit http://www.harvest.org/knowgod.

APPENDIX
The Plan of Salvation

1. The Condition: We Are All Sinners

The first thing we need to establish with those whom we share the gospel is the fact that we all are sinners. One word that defines sin is the Greek word *harmatia*, which means "to miss the mark." What is God's mark? Perfection. Jesus said, "Be perfect, therefore, as your heavenly Father is perfect" (Matthew 5:48 NIV). Apart from God, no one is perfect; everyone has missed the mark. Therefore, everyone is a sinner.

- *1 John 1:8–9:* "If we say that we have no sin, we deceive ourselves, and the truth is not in us. If we confess our sins, He is faithful and just to forgive us our sins and to cleanse us from all unrighteousness."

- *Romans 3:23:* "For all have sinned and fall short of the glory of God."

- *Isaiah 53:6:* "All we like sheep have gone astray; we have turned, every one, to his own way; and the Lord has laid on Him the iniquity of us all."

2. The Result: Death

Next, we need to establish the result of sin. Every one of us has missed God's mark. Every one of us has fallen short of being perfect. The result of that is death. We are getting only what we deserve, and we are bringing that judgment upon ourselves. One thing we need to remember is that God does not send anyone to hell. We send ourselves there by rejecting His truth.

- *Romans 6:23:* "For the wages of sin is death, but the gift of God is eternal life in Christ Jesus our Lord."

3. The Solution: Christ's Death on the Cross

At this point, let people know the solution: Christ died for our sins.

- *John 3:16–17:* " 'For God so loved the world that He gave His only begotten Son, that whoever believes in Him should not perish but have everlasting life. For God did not send His Son into the world to condemn the world, but that the world through Him might be saved.' "

- *Isaiah 53:5:* "He was wounded for our transgressions, He was bruised for our iniquities; the chastisement for our peace was upon Him, and by His stripes we are healed."

- *Romans 5:8:* "God demonstrates His own love toward us, in that while we were still sinners, Christ died for us."

Since we can never measure up to God's standards on our own, God has reached out to us. We cannot solve the problem of sin, but God, who is perfect, can and has. He has become a bridge for us through Jesus Christ.

4. The Choice: To Accept or Reject Jesus Christ as Savior

If someone will acknowledge they are sinners and accept the premise that Christ is the solution, they are at a crossroads. Either they can reject God's solution and accept the consequences, or they can accept Jesus Christ as Savior. What must they do to be forgiven of their sins and come into a relationship with God?

First, they must repent.

- *Luke 13:3:* " 'I tell you, no; but unless you repent you will all likewise perish.' "

- *Acts 3:19:* " 'Repent therefore and be converted, that your sins may be blotted out, so that times of refreshing may come from the presence of the Lord.' "

- *Acts 17:30:* " 'Truly these times of ignorance God overlooked, but now commands all men everywhere to repent.' "

Upon the realization that he or she is a sinner and has repented of that sin, an individual must then come to Jesus Christ.

- *Matthew 11:28–30:* " 'Come to Me, all you who labor and are heavy laden, and I will give you rest. Take My yoke upon you and learn from Me, for I am gentle and lowly in heart, and you will find rest for your souls. For My yoke is easy and My burden is light.' "

5. The Response: To Receive the Gift of Eternal Life

Christ's invitation is clear. We must come to Him. All that remains is a response.

- *Romans 6:23:* "For the wages of sin is death, but the gift of God is eternal life in Christ Jesus our Lord."

What must we do to receive God's gift of salvation? Take it!

- *Revelation 3:20:* " 'Behold, I stand at the door and knock. If anyone hears My voice and opens the door, I will come in to him and dine with him, and he with Me.' "

Jesus stands at the door of your heart and mine and knocks, seeking entrance into our lives. What do we have to do to let Him in? Open the door!

- *John 1:12:* "But as many as received Him, to them He gave the right to become children of God, to those who believe in His name."

We must receive Him. How? By asking Him into our lives.

If we have shared these truths with an unbeliever and he or she wants to receive Christ, then we need only to extend the invitation. In fact, we should pray with the individual at that very moment if he or she would like to make this life-changing decision to receive and follow Jesus Christ. I know of no greater joy than leading someone in a prayer to receive Christ.

6. The Assurance of Salvation

Following this, it is important that a new believer has the assurance that Christ has come into his or her life.

- *1 John 5:11–13:* "And this is the testimony: that God has given us eternal life, and this life is in His Son. He who has the Son has life; he who does not have the Son of God does not have life. These things I have written to you who believe in the name of the Son of God, that you may know that you have eternal life, and that you may continue to believe in the name of the Son of God."

- *2 Corinthians 5:17:* "Therefore, if anyone is in Christ, he is a new creation; old things have passed away; behold, all things have become new."

- *Psalm 103:12:* "As far as the east is from the west, so far has He removed our transgressions from us."

7. The Profession of Faith

At this time, you may encourage a new believer to make a public confession of his or her newfound faith in Christ.

- *Matthew 10:32–33:* " 'Therefore whoever confesses Me before men, him I will also confess before My Father who is in heaven. But whoever denies Me before men, him I will also deny before My Father who is in heaven.' "

After you have led someone to Christ, it is important to take them under your wing and help them get established in their relationship with Christ.

Notes

1. Ray Stedman, "The Coming of Joy," *The Ray C. Stedman Library;* http://www.raystedman.org/misc/3018.html

2. Abraham Lincoln, J. T. Hobson, comp., *The Lincoln Yearbook* (Dayton, Ohio: United Brethren Publishing House, 1912), 197.

3. Martin Luther, Martin E. Marty, ed., *The Place of Trust: Martin Luther on the Sermon on the Mount* (New York: Harper & Row, Publishers, 1983), 34.

Other AllenDavid Books Published by Kerygma Publishing

Visit:

www.kerygmapublishing.com
www.allendavidbooks.com